the

parent soup

A-to-Z Guide
to Your
New Baby

advice that works from parents who've been there—
from anger to pacifiers to weaning

Kate Hanley & the Parents of Parent Soup
Medical Information from Dr. Alan Greene
Foreword by Nancy Evans

CB
CONTEMPORARY BOOKS

Library of Congress Cataloging-in-Publication Data

Hanley, Kate.
    The parent soup a-to-z guide to your new baby : advice that works from
parents who've been there—from anger to pacifiers to weaning / Kate
Hanley & the parents of Parent Soup ; foreword by Nancy Evans.
       p.   cm.
    ISBN 0-8092-2960-9
       1. Infants (Newborn)—Care—Popular works.   2. Infants (Newborn)—
Health and hygiene—Popular works.   I. Parent Soup.   II. Title.
RJ253.H36   1998
649'.122—DC21   97-50256
                                                               CIP

Every effort has been made to ensure the accuracy of this book. We cannot,
however, guarantee that the advice in this book will work for you. It should be
used for informational purposes only. This book is in no way intended to replace
or supersede qualified medical or other professional care. If you or your child is
experiencing a medical problem, please consult your physician. The authors and
publishers encourage you to get appropriate medical care and disclaim any
liability resulting from the use of this book.

Interior design by Maria Garcia-Palencia
Interior production by Susan H. Hartman
Associate producer: Felicia Jones

Published by Contemporary Books
A division of NTC/Contemporary Publishing Group, Inc.
4255 West Touhy Avenue, Lincolnwood (Chicago), Illinois 60646-1975 U.S.A.
Copyright © 1998 by iVillage Inc.

Printed in the United States of America
International Standard Book Number: 0-8092-2960-9
98   99   00   01   02   03   QP   11   10   9   8   7   6   5   4   3   2   1

foreword

If you ask the mothers (and fathers) who use Parent Soup what they like best about it, they answer: "Us." What they mean—and what you'll soon discover in this book—is that they like the parents they've met through Parent Soup, the advice they've gotten, the support they've received, the camaraderie they've shared, and the laughs they've had. This is where they go to make contact with another mom or dad any time of the day or night.

No mom needs and uses Parent Soup more than the new mom, and as a new mom you can understand this. You now have more questions than at almost any other time in your life—and less mobility than at any other time. Parent Soup meets both needs, answers and access, with thousands of parents ready to answer your every question (including moms who have already made it through babyhood) literally there at your fingertips. Turn on your computer, click to go online, and you can find them there *live*: real moms and dads you can talk to this very instant. You can talk to them in a chat room or you can type a message ("My baby isn't sleeping through the night; help!"), and answers will come within moments, sometimes over the next days and weeks. The feeling is (and what a relief this is) that you're not alone, that you've got a friend. You've got a whole lot of friends—in fact, an entire community.

In this book you'll find support and advice on a host of subjects dear to the new mother's heart, coming from other new mothers who have gone or are going through the very things you are. You can read advice on how to breastfeed (Parent Soup has breastfeeding moms online while they are nursing—one hand cradling the baby, the other hand typing on the keyboard!) and when to introduce solid foods. You can find discussions about loving a baby too much and loving a husband too little. And let's talk about sleep or the lack thereof and sex or the lack thereof. As Parent Soup members often say, "I feel better just knowing I'm not alone"—not alone in being tired, in being worried, in not having all the answers!

Along with the wisdom of mothers, you'll also find straightforward answers from Parent Soup's resident pediatrician, Dr. Alan Greene. He's a dad of four, a practicing pediatrician in San Mateo, and a published author. And because his name is Dr. Greene, he wears green socks, which make the kids who come to see him smile. He has office hours every day at Parent Soup. He's there at the Soup, as he is in this book, to answer the questions that only a doctor who keeps up on the latest research can appropriately answer.

We think you'll find this book a comfort. It isn't simply a book to read through and then put up on a shelf but a companion to see you through the first year of motherhood. Add your own active participation at Parent Soup to supplement what we've already gathered here from our community, and you will feel surrounded and supported by the collective mother's love that every mother needs. You've got a friend—a whole bunch of friends—here at Parent Soup.

Nancy Evans

~ *Nancy Evans   nancy@iVillage.com*

parent soup is part of
iVillage.com
THE WOMEN'S NETWORK

parent soup

acknowledgments

the book you're holding in your hands is a true collaboration—many people in many places contributed to the final product, and I am indebted to them all. Many thanks to Kaitlyn Simpson, Tory Crimmins, Fern Thomas, Kevin McAuliffe, Brett Joubert, Laurie Petersen, Lori Nelson, Joan Chakonas, Madeline Sumera, Cynthia Schmae, Kate Powers, Magalie JJ Lawrence, and Janice Fredrick for volunteering their spare time (!) to read posts from parents on the Parent Soup message boards; Susan Weaver, Jackie Needleman, and Christina Ohly for calm assistance in pulling information together as the deadline loomed large; the entire Parent Soup staff for their help in gathering vital pieces of the puzzle; Bill Moulton for his design skills; Dr. Alan and Cheryl Greene for their enthusiastic and thoughtful contributions; Felicia Jones for her day-to-day support and hard work; and Nancy Evans for her immeasurable editorial guidance and vision.

I would also like to recognize Susan Hahn, Noni Byrnes, Anne Marie Mackin, and Tarrant Figlio—they are all Parent Soup community leaders who use their extensive collective parenting wisdom and knack for making others comfortable to keep Parent Soup a warm and helpful place. You'll see quotes from these wise women throughout the book. They are a vital part of Parent Soup's recipe, and I am grateful for their knowledge and support.

~ K.H.

introduction

You may be wondering, "Who is Parent Soup and why are they telling me how to raise my baby?" Parent Soup is an online gathering place on AOL and the Web where thousands of parents talk to each other every day, lend a helping hand, and engage in conversations with parenting experts of all types. Because there's no parent alive who can't use help raising a child, and because there's no better source of advice and comfort than other parents, Parent Soup is an ideal parenting tool for these modern times.

When we polled parents at our Parent Soup Web site, we found that only 20 percent of people felt immediately comfortable and competent in their new role as parent. So for the other 80 percent of you, we offer this book as a resource and a comfort as you learn the ropes. This book incorporates the best of the Soup—collective wisdom from parents across the country, expert advice, informative poll questions, and brainteaser trivia questions. You'll hear from La Leche League International (LLLI) on all matters related to breast-feeding and from the Dependent Care Connection on how to find good child care. Within these pages, you'll also meet Dr. Alan Greene, our resident pediatrician, and learn his thoughtful, sensible approach to parenting.

A practicing pediatrician in San Mateo, California, Dr. Greene views each child as an individual and encourages parents and child-care providers to see children as unique and deserving of individualized care and attention. He has impeccable qualifications. Dr. Greene attended Princeton University as an undergraduate and went on to the top-ranked medical school at the University of California San Francisco. He was Chief Resident at the Children's Hospital Medical Center of Northern California and passed the Pediatric Boards in the top 5 percent nationwide. On the Voluntary Clinical Faculty at Stanford University, he was awarded the "Physician's Recognition Award" by the American Medical Association. He's the author of two books: *The Parent's Complete Guide to Ear Infections* and *A Pound of Prevention— 16 Things You Can Do to Give Your Child a Long and Healthy Life.* His love of children is evident, and he and his wife, Cheryl, have four healthy kids of their own. Dr. Greene appears regularly at Parent Soup to chat with parents. And in his spare time (you may be asking, "What spare time?") Dr. Greene teaches each of his children to play chess!

But what's really important here are the voices of the parents of Parent Soup. Every single person who's quoted in this book has at one time or another been overwhelmed by being a parent, and they all have found something—a trick to soothing their baby, a reassuring thought, a little tidbit of information—that has helped them through it. In their voices you'll hear compassion, wisdom, and humor that can give you solace as well as information. But the most important thing this book can do is reassure you that you are not alone on your parenting journey.

The topics covered here apply to caring for yourself (dealing with the stress caused by a crying baby, postpartum depression, and mother love) as well as caring for your baby (diapering, bottle-feeding, and sleeping). We know that a big part of having a happy and healthy baby is being a happy and healthy parent, and that becoming a parent is one of the strangest, hardest jobs you'll ever have.

We've organized the information so that it's as easy as possible to find what you need while one hand is occupied holding the baby. All subjects are arranged alphabetically, and we've designed the book so that the most important ideas are highlighted and that the information from the experts is set off in a different format from the content that came from our members.

Everything you see in this book has been fact-checked. For instance, when one Parent Soup member wrote that she called Enfamil to see how long formula was good, we called Enfamil and double-checked. [We spoke to Sue, who was quite friendly; she can be reached at (800) 222-9123.] Dr. Greene also read the tips from parents to make sure that all their suggestions are safe. Still, we must advise you that while all remedies suggested in this book have worked for someone, we cannot promise they will all work for you. One of the most important lessons to learn from the parents featured on these pages is that finding a successful parenting style comes only through experimentation. You must discover what works best for you and your baby.

So here are some ideas to get you started. And we hope that as you figure out what works and what doesn't work for you and your family, you'll come online and share it with our community and help us carry on the tradition of passionate parenting.

~ Kate Hanley   hanley@iVillage.com

ANGER *(See also Crying and Colic)*

Learning to live with a new baby is wonderful, but it is also sure to cause some frustration (new babies change everything!). That frustration is often the root of anger. If you're feeling you're about to spin out of control in the face of yet another round of screaming or the 37th spit up of the day, take a step back.

First, remember that humans—babies—learn what they see. And that means if your baby sees you obviously flustered, he will likely follow suit. The calmer you are, the calmer your baby will be. If you aren't sure you can keep your cool in front of the baby, hand him off to your partner or caregiver and leave the room for a minute. Take your own version of Time Out: Breathe deeply. Collect your thoughts. And remind yourself that your frustration does not make you a bad parent. It makes you human.

Getting Perspective

I love my baby with all my heart and soul, but when he cries incessantly at 2:00 A.M., I get annoyed. It's only natural, and I'll admit that I don't hold the monopoly on patience. But no matter how tired or angry I am, I smile at that baby and I thank God from the bottom of my heart that he's there to cry. I hold him, rock him, and talk softly for hours if I need to until he calms down. I know he'll calm down much faster and feel much better if I don't lose my temper. If, one day, I ever get to the point where I feel I can't control my temper, I will put him down and leave the room until I have control of myself.

~ *Lisa M., Dearborn, Michigan*

> **DR. GREENE'S INSIGHT:** Don't tell my kids, but even I get frustrated with my kids sometimes. The thing to remember is that we don't need to be perfect in order to be great parents.

Don't Keep Up with the Joneses

Don't get all upset over a few Super Parents whose mottoes are "I'm perfect, and so are my kids," and "You're not as good as I am." Any parent who says he hasn't had a bad day with the kids, who hasn't ever lost his composure and said or thought something he didn't mean, is either a liar or has comatose kids. You just have to hang in there and take it one day at a time, and always start each day anew. Don't dwell on or get the guilts over a bad day the day before.

~ *Bill, Minnesota*

> **DR. GREENE'S INSIGHT:** I think the hardest thing is that kids often don't respect our favorite possessions. It's not so much that we like things more than kids, but that their lack of care is frustrating. Respecting our kids and their concerns is the quickest path toward teaching them to respect ours.

Remember What's Important

Don't have anything in your home that is more important than your child. It is a horrible thing for children to grow up thinking that if they break this or that, their parents won't love them anymore. Your kids may be too young to pick up on this yet, but it's never too early to develop a healthy attitude toward raising kids. I was a nanny for a woman with a white carpet. She had a fit if there was the slightest spot on the carpet. And the children grew up feeling that the carpet was more important than they were. It's important for us all to remember that *nothing* (especially carpet) is more valuable than our children.

~ *Tarrant F., Eugene, Oregon*

BABY-PROOFING

When you bring your baby home from the hospital, suddenly the fireplace you once thought was so cozy becomes a potential hazard. There are many products marketed to parents to baby-proof their homes, but you don't have to buy every one of them. As with most parenting issues, the best solutions often rely on common sense. Below are Parent Soup's 17 most popular and practical ways to make your home safe for your new arrival.

1. Crawl through your house to get a baby's-eye view, and remove anything that is either dangerous to your baby or precious to you.

2. Turn down your hot water heater to 120 degrees Fahrenheit to prevent burns.

3. Secure cupboard doors with childproof locks—but don't expect them to work all the time (some babies are more wily than others!). Put dangerous items (e.g., cleaning solutions, knives) in high cabinets, far out of the reach of children. Leave one easy-to-reach cupboard open and fill it with plastic containers or pots and pans that are safe for baby to play with.

4. Cover all electrical sockets with plastic plugs or, better yet, replace the cover plates with childproof ones.

5. Take the sharp edges off your fireplace or furniture by covering them with throw pillows, quilts, blankets, or foam rubber. Murphy's Law dictates that falls will happen in the worst-possible places.

b baby-proofing

TRIVIA QUESTION

What is the safety product most commonly purchased by new parents?

a. Plug and outlet covers

b. Cord shorteners

c. Security gates

d. Cabinet locks

e. Waterspout covers

Answer: a

From *Parent Soup: The Game* (Source: Bruni and Ridgway Research Associates, Inc.)

6. Put a hook-and-eye latch high up on your doors so that baby doesn't end up anywhere he shouldn't be (like the basement or outside).

7. Make sure every area of your house has a smoke detector and a carbon monoxide detector. If you need help or information, call your local fire station.

8. Remove refrigerator magnets. They frequently fall off the refrigerator when the door is slammed, and they are small enough to pose a choking risk.

9. Program your phone's speed dial with the numbers of your pediatrician, the poison control center, your partner at work, and your ambulance service (if you don't have 911). Let your baby-sitter know the numbers are there.

10. Keep a bottle of ipecac syrup on hand (up high or in a locked cabinet, of course) in case of poisoning emergency. This syrup is derived from a plant of the same name, and it triggers vomiting (not all poison cases require vomiting, so be sure to check with a doctor before administering it). Call your local poison control center for an emergency reference card. Let your baby-sitter know where the syrup and card are.

11. Keep older siblings' toys separate, either in their room or in a playpen, so that your baby can't get at them.

12. Make sure your baby monitor works and is within range. As a test place a ticking clock near it. If you can hear the tick-tock, you can be sure you'll hear the baby.

13. Keep hot liquids away from baby. Whenever you're drinking coffee, tea, or other hot liquids, be sure to keep the drink far enough away so that if it spills, your baby won't get burned.

14. Never leave your baby alone in the bath. Babies can drown in just inches of water, so always stay next to your baby when you're bathing her (or when you're near a pool, the toilet, or a bucket of water). If the phone rings, let the machine get it—or buy and use a cordless phone.

15. Don't expose your baby to smoke. Secondhand smoke can cause illness now and serious health problems down the road.

16. Ask a professional. In many areas, professional "baby-proofers" will come to your home, install protectors and locks, and look for hazards you might not notice. Because they are so quick, they can be inexpensive. Ask your pediatrician if there are any reliable, inexpensive baby-proofers in your area.

17. Get a good stain stick to clean anything that you didn't baby-proof.

BATHING

Changing a wriggly baby is challenge enough. How are you supposed to handle a wet, slippery baby at bath time? And how often does a baby need to be bathed? Parent Soup's resident pediatrician Dr. Alan Greene has some great tips on bathing your baby.

How Do I Bathe My Baby?

Q: I am 22 years old and a brand-new mom. There's so much I don't know! How do I give my little girl a bath? She's so tiny—what if I drop her? What kind of soap do I use? When does she need a bath? Today on the phone my mom asked me how bath time was going. She was shocked when I told her I hadn't given Emily a bath yet (she's four days old). Please help!

 ~ *Jeanne, Lemoore, California*

DR. GREENE'S INSIGHT

A: You (and your mother) will be glad to know that Emily has probably already had her first minibath a short time after delivery. In the hospital nursery a skilled nurse carefully laid her on a table (not unlike a kitchen or bathroom sink countertop that is very, very clean) and cradled her head in one hand. With the other hand she gently washed Emily with a warm (not hot) washcloth without soap. As soon as the bath was over, the nurse put a clean diaper on your baby and wrapped her in a warm blanket. Until the umbilical stump has fallen off and the belly button is dry, you, too, can follow this pattern. For a circumcised boy you can follow this pattern until his penis has healed from the surgery.

Other Sponge-Bathing Tips

- It doesn't matter what time of the day you bathe your baby. Babies adapt well to different times of the day for baths, though many enjoy a bath right before bed.

- Select a convenient place. I mentioned using a kitchen or bathroom counter. You may also want to try a changing table or bed.

- Cover the area with a thick towel or waterproof pad if needed.

- Get everything you will need ready *before* you start! The supply list includes water (of course), washcloth, rubbing-alcohol pads, bath towel (with hood if you have one), clean diaper, any items you routinely use during a diaper change, and fresh clothes. I do not recommend using soap or shampoo on newborn babies. And if this is her first bath, you may want to get out the camera.

- Babies lose body heat very quickly, so make sure the room is warm—75 to 80 degrees Fahrenheit is ideal.

- Gently cradle your baby's head in one hand, and use the other hand to remove her clothing.

- Wash her with a soft, warm washcloth, and dry her off with a towel. If you like, you can put a fresh item of clothing on as soon as an area is washed and dried. This is not necessary unless you are in a chilly room.

b bathing

- Be sure to gently wash behind her ears; in the crevices in her neck, elbows, and knees; and in between her fingers and toes.

- Wash your newborn's hair near the end of the bath time. This will help prevent her from losing too much body heat. Most newborns don't have much hair, so it is easy to sponge it with water, much the same way as you do the rest of the body. Almost all babies dislike getting their eyes wet: if you tip the head back just a bit and work your way from the front to the back, you can avoid this.

- Leave the diaper area until last. When you do get to it, remove her diaper and sponge off the skin on her belly and bottom. Usually babies' genitals need only gentle cleansing. With little girls, wash from the front to the back. Don't be concerned if you see a white discharge or vaginal bleeding. These are both normal for newborn girls, and the discharge does not need to be wiped away completely. Leave whatever does not come off with one gentle pass. If you have a son, do not retract or pull back the foreskin on an uncircumcised penis. Do not wash the head of a circumcised penis before it is healed.

- Before putting a clean diaper on your baby, gently raise the umbilical stump and clean around the bottom of the stump with a rubbing-alcohol pad.

- Dress your fresh, clean, and oh-so-cuddly baby.

Some babies love bath time, though that is unusual. Most babies are a bit frightened by the experience of having their clothes taken off and being exposed to the air. *If your baby loves her bath, feel free to make it part of your daily routine. If she doesn't love it, it isn't necessary to bathe her daily.* As long as you are changing her diaper regularly, cleaning her diaper area after poops (I don't recommend using prepared wipes that contain alcohol, soap, or perfumes), and spot cleaning after spit ups, she shouldn't need to be bathed more often than every three or four days. If she starts to smell, you will know it's time for her bath!

If your baby's skin is drying out too much, you will want to cut back on the frequency of baths and apply an alcohol-free, unscented baby lotion daily—especially after each bath.

Tub Bathing

After the baby's umbilical stump falls off (that is, after two to four weeks) and her belly button is dry, she will be ready for a tub bath. By that time you will feel like a pro, and you will be able to adapt the ideas I've already outlined to tub bathing. There are, however, a few additional things to point out:

- Use a tub that is the right size for your baby. Most baby tubs you can purchase come with an insert for young babies. This makes it much easier for you to keep your child's head out of the water.

- Never, *never* leave your baby alone in a bath! Don't even leave her long enough to answer the phone or turn off the stove. If you remember that you left the stove on in the middle of bath time, take your baby out of the bath, wrap her in a towel, and take her with you into the kitchen to turn off the stove. On your way back to the bath, grab a dry towel to use when her bath is complete.

- You need to use only a couple of inches of water in the tub, and make sure the water is warm, not hot. A baby's skin is very sensitive to heat. If you are unsure about a safe temperature, you can buy an inexpensive bath thermometer at a local baby store or drugstore. These simple devices change color to indicate safe and unsafe heat levels.

- Gentle soaps really are better for a baby's skin during the first year or so. (Note: Ivory is *not* a gentle soap. Try an unscented baby soap or Dove, Basis, or Neutrogena.) Use soap sparingly and avoid scrubbing.

- Don't use adult shampoo on your baby. The no-tears advertisements for baby shampoos are for real.

- Make bath time fun. Use age-appropriate toys to engage your baby in the whole experience. At first this might be something as simple as giving her a clean washcloth to suck on during the bath. Later, plastic cups and bowls make excellent pouring toys.

Transition to Tub

If your baby is sitting up by herself, bathe her in that big ol' bathtub in your bathroom. She will love it! Add only about an inch and a half of water and put a bath towel on the bottom to protect her; then let her go. If she isn't sitting by herself, the bath rings made by Fisher Price are  great. I used one for my second child so I could bathe her with my oldest and not have to have my hand on her every second. It worked really well and she loved taking baths with her big sister.

~ *Angela K., South Bound Brook, New Jersey*

Not Fancy, Just Functional

I purchased a square, very strong plastic laundry basket from Target a
couple of years ago to hold toys. But now I've discovered it makes a great
minibath for my eight-month-old. With my baby in the basket, I can
bathe my four-year-old child and baby together, and I don't have to
worry about them slipping and sliding into each other. I love it!

~ *Megan, Minnesota*

One to Grow On

My baby doesn't like to be restrained, so I didn't even try a bath seat
when she outgrew the kitchen sink. I got a toddler tub; it fits inside the
regular bathtub, is easy to rinse out when finished, and still fits my now
16-month-old and her many tub toys.

~ *Parent Soup member TomF999*

The Bath Ring

If you're wondering how to get your baby's bottom clean when using a
bath ring, you simply wash the entire body and save his bottom for last.
Then you lift the little one out of the seat, lean him over one arm, and
wash away with your free hand.

~ *Lisa L., Jax, Florida*

Baby Odor

Baby odor is sometimes caused by a fungus that grows in the folds of the
neck and armpits. This can be treated using a cream such as Lotrimin
after bathing. My daughter (now almost six months old) had that problem
for a while, but now that she's more upright (better air circulation?) and
has lost a little of the baby fat under her chin, it seems to have cleared up.

~ *Laurie H., Alameda, California*

My daughter had this problem, too. She was a regular Michelin baby, and it was just plain hard to dry in between all those folds. We applied cornstarch to keep the problem areas dry.

~ *Lisa K., Tucker, Georgia*

BITING *(See also Teething)*

You know how a baby can sit and stare at his hand for hours? It's because he's fascinated by his own body and how it works. As he gets older and more coordinated, he also learns how to put his body to use, finding out what each part is for. At some point or another he will start experimenting with all the different ways to use his mouth (food processor, communication device, musical instrument). The chances are good that he will start biting down on anything that holds still. When what he bites is another human being (probably you, and probably while he's nursing), he will learn that he gets a reaction, which he may start to like. His reaction is fixable with the right approach—a combination of gentle discipline and distraction. Here are some ideas for coping with unwanted biting.

Give Them Something to Chew On

My kids went through a biting phase. Someone told me that biting isn't always a sign of aggression and that sometimes kids just need something to bite. I gave mine frozen bagels or frozen teething rings and said, "If you want to bite, here is something you can bite." It was enough to distract them and get them to stop gnawing on each other.

~ *Bev B., Studio City, California*

When a Baby Bites the Breast That Feeds Her

Q: Help!! I am still nursing my nine-month-old and thoroughly enjoy it.
However, in the past two weeks she has taken to biting me when we
are nursing. I think she thinks it's a game because she smiles when I
jump. I don't know how to teach her to stop—it is not fun!!

~ *Aline M., Fernandina Beach, Florida*

La Leche League Responds

A: There are many mothers out there who have experienced the
aggravation of a baby who discovers biting. Be assured your daughter
cannot bite and nurse at the same time because the two actions
require different movements. One solution that some mothers have
found to be successful is to firmly but quietly say, "No biting!" and
take the baby off the breast. Do not allow the baby to resume nursing
for a little while. Your daughter will quickly discover that you are not
going to allow this behavior.

Another helpful hint is to keep a finger close by, ready to pop in
her mouth and stop the bite as she clamps down. This will keep you
from getting hurt and allow you to deal with the situation without a
reaction. Most babies will give up biting very quickly when they
discover that mom is not going to let them get away with it and that
they can't get a reaction.

BOTTLE-FEEDING
(See also Breastfeeding—Difficulty)

Mothers who bottle-feed don't love their babies any less than
mothers who breastfeed. They just have more stuff in their diaper bags.

b bottle-feeding

As Parent Soup member Jamie97735 so wisely reminds mothers who feel guilty about not breastfeeding, "Remember that many happy, healthy babies have been bottle-fed."

Learning what to do with all the various bottles, nipples, formulas, and combinations thereof may seem daunting, but it's really not (at least not when you've got parents from across the country to help you out).

One Parent Soup participant asked these basic questions.

Q: My six-week-old baby is on formula, and I have many questions:

- How long can you leave a bottle out and still use its contents? Is this different for powdered and for ready-to-feed formulas?

- Is there a limit on how many times you can heat up the same bottle? I don't want to subject my baby to bacteria, but formula is so expensive; she doesn't always finish the bottle, and I don't want to waste it!

- Is there a super bottle that *really* reduces gas, and I just don't know about it?
   ~ Parent Soup member NiteKryme

Reheating Formula and Avoiding Gas

A: When I first started bottle-feeding, I had a million questions! Maybe some of what I learned can help you. As for how long formula is good, I called Enfamil and a representative said formula is good for up to two hours (total) unrefrigerated, as long as the bottle remains unused. Once the baby starts eating, the formula is good for a total of only one hour. Throw away any leftover and do not reheat the formula. As for nipples, my son was very particular. Avent nipples were the only ones he'd take.

You also have to be sure to push all the air out before your baby drinks, try to burp every one-and-a-half to two ounces, and sit upright after feeding (it makes those elusive burps come up easier). I have also found powdered formula tends to cause more gas in my baby, and I now give him only ready-to-feed. Last, but not least, if your baby continues to have gas, you may want to change formulas. We had to try a couple before we found one that worked.

> DR. GREENE'S INSIGHT: Avent nipples are great—we used them with our youngest. But different babies prefer different nipples. Yours might prefer ones made by Johnson & Johnson or Playtex. Isn't it amazing how particular babies can be?

~ *Parent Soup member FSUkitty*

Serving Size and Concentrated or Powdered Formula

A: If your baby isn't finishing a whole bottle of formula, you might try decreasing the amount you put in each bottle. I usually used the concentrated formula, but I made it a point to give my babies the powdered formula once in a while so they became used to both. I liked using the powder for day trips out so I didn't have to take along chilled bottles and then worry about having them heated. I would just fill a couple of bottles with hot water and add the powder when the baby was hungry.

~ *Angela K., South Bound Brook, New Jersey*

Hot or Cold Formula?

A: If you want to feed your baby cold formula, don't ask your mother-in-law! She will tell you that cold milk gives the baby a tummy ache. It doesn't. I asked my doctor. While many babies prefer their milk

b bottle-feeding

LOVING YOUR DECISION TO BOTTLE-FEED

The most important thing is that if you decide for any reason not to breastfeed, it is OK and you do not have to explain yourself to anyone. It's your decision, and your baby will be just fine on formula. Do not beat yourself up about it. What matters is that mommy and baby are happy and content.

*~ Angela K.,
South Bound
Brook, New Jersey*

warm, mine didn't. He's three now, and I never warmed his bottles— and he did just fine.

~ Chris, California

Sterilize Every Bottle?

Q: My sister-in-law says that she only needs to sterilize the bottles once every two weeks. Otherwise, she can just use soap and hot water. Is she out of her mind or have times changed?

~ Parent Soup member USFChick

A: Sterilization is no longer considered necessary. Good washing with soap and water or running them through the dishwasher is sufficient. The only time you should sterilize the bottles and nipples is when the child is ill, so you don't keep reinfecting him.

~Tarrant F., Eugene, Oregon

Is Baby Getting Enough?

Q: I have a healthy, happy three-month-old boy. He weighs 16 pounds and is nice and solid. But I'm worried about him. I must be paying too much attention to what the experts say about how much formula he should consume a day, because I'm scared he's not taking enough (not even 30 ounces a day). Am I crazy?

~ Page S., Houston, Texas

A: I was having the same problem with my baby the first few months— worrying and counting the ounces he did or did not drink. I think the best advice is to *stop* counting!

Your baby is apparently doing just fine, as evidenced by his weight. If not keeping track makes you nervous, just try it for a week or two; then get him weighed at the doctor's. If he's gaining, you can be confident that you don't have to worry about how much he drinks. As my mother-in-law says, "The baby is smarter than you are and he knows what to do."

~ *Elizabeth I., Chicago, Illinois*

> DR. GREENE'S INSIGHT: After all, breast-feeding moms can't count how much their babies are eating.

BREASTFEEDING

Contrary to the belief in place when many of us were babies, breastfeeding is now considered the best way to feed your baby. Breast milk is specifically formulated to sustain and foster human babies, and it has been doing so with great success since the beginning of time. Among its proved benefits are a lower risk of infections in babies, a reduced risk of breast cancer in mothers, and monetary savings to parents (both on food and medical bills, as breastfed babies have to see the doctor less often). We learn more about the amazing components of breast milk all the time. Despite all these benefits, breastfeeding isn't always easy. But now there are organizations, such as La Leche League, and communities of breastfeeders, such as the ones at Parent Soup, to answer the questions each breastfeeding mother invariably has.

Increasing Milk Supply

Q: I have left the working world to be at home for a while. My milk supply has decreased a lot because I was only nursing a few times a day. How can I get my milk supply increased again to satisfy my hungry five-month-old?

~ *Elisa, Ohio*

A: Drink lots of water all day. Be sure you are eating enough and getting rest (very difficult!). It's hard to relax when you are so busy, but try some relaxation exercises or just taking a warm bath or shower to encourage a let down. Just a thought—are you on birth control pills? Without knowing the side effects, I went back on the pill after my son was born, while still breastfeeding him, and noticed a severe decrease in my milk supply. I quit the pill after one month, and my supply returned, thank goodness.

~ *Constance I., El Paso, Texas*

A: The basic concept with increasing your milk is based on the supply and demand theory. The more you nurse and the more the baby is asking your body for, the more your body will respond to this request and produce more mik. It can take a couple of days, but it will come back once the baby nurses more.

~ *Parent Soup member NTZAN*

La Leche League Responds
A: Let's review some of the basic principles of a baby's weight gain and increasing your milk supply. The amount of milk the mother produces depends on the frequency and effectiveness of the sucking that the baby does at the breast. Is your baby waking at night to nurse? Is the baby's suck strong? Do you hear swallowing? These are indications that the baby is nursing often enough.

At about three months the baby often goes through a growth spurt, when he may build up the mother's milk supply through fussiness, an increased need to nurse, or both. It would be normal for the baby to have a temporarily increased need to nurse at this stage.

A baby usually gains four to eight ounces a week during the first three months.

As you may know, supplementing with formula can interfere with the process of supply and demand, causing the baby to take less from the breast so that the mother's milk supply decreases. Because artificial baby milk is not digested as quickly or completely as human milk, it can leave baby feeling full longer. You and your doctor should look carefully at how much weight your baby is gaining and ways to improve your breastfeeding management so you can gradually reduce the supplements.

(To learn more about some of these suggestions, turn to the Resources section to find a La Leche League chapter near you.)

Different Milk at Different Times

Q: I've noticed that my six-month-old son nurses more frequently in the morning than in the afternoon. I have also noticed that when I express my milk in the morning, it is much more watery and thin, like skim milk, and in the afternoon it looks more like 2 percent milk (white and thick). Is this normal?

~ *Parent Soup member Gring17813*

La Leche League Responds

A: What you are asking about is perfectly normal! Milk supply is highest in the morning, and it tapers off gradually during the day as a baby takes what's needed. It is lowest in the evening hours after baby has had a day of nursing. Your body tires and, hence, does not produce as much milk.

As you mentioned, the milk is thinner and more watery in the morning and seems thicker and whiter later in the day. The thinner milk is the *foremilk*, which has been stored up overnight. It quenches the baby's thirst. The *hindmilk* is the thick, rich, creamy, white milk you noticed. It is richer than the foremilk, and the baby doesn't need as much of it to feel satisfied. This may be the reason he doesn't nurse as much later in the day.

Making Sure Baby Gets Enough

Q: My husband and I recently had our first baby. I am trying to breastfeed exclusively, but the baby is refusing my breast at times.

PARENT POLL

Is it OK to breastfeed in public?

Of 1,076 total votes

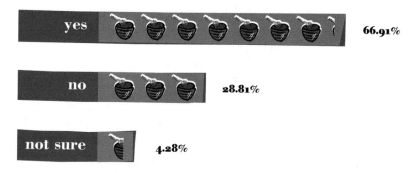

yes   66.91%

no   28.81%

not sure   4.28%

1 bowl = 100 parents

She will latch on and then pull away and scream. My husband and I are both getting concerned about her appetite. I am not sure how much she does eat. Any input would be appreciated.

~ *Barbara K., Sarasota, Florida*

La Leche League Responds

A: It's always hard to determine how much a breastfed baby is eating when there are no markings on a bottle to measure intake. The best way to determine that your daughter is getting enough breast milk is to watch for six to eight wet diapers a day and two or more bowel movements.

> **DR. GREENE'S INSIGHT:** Some healthy, well-fed babies urinate only three or four times a day and poop only once every several days.

As for the baby refusing the breast sometimes and pulling off and screaming, it's possible your daughter is frustrated and so hungry that she can't settle down to wait for the milk to let down after she starts nursing. Try to nurse your daughter before she gets too hungry, about every two to three hours. If your daughter is still frustrated and pulling off, you can try walking and nursing, which calms down some babies.

BREASTFEEDING—DIFFICULTY
(See also Postpartum Depression)

Sometimes breastfeeding just doesn't work. Your baby may not latch on properly; your milk might let down too fast or not fast enough. The things that can go wrong are myriad. If you're having trouble breast-feeding, you are not alone: the voices at Parent Soup attest to that. But if you are determined to make it work, here are some strategies that have worked for others to make breastfeeding a successful endeavor; perhaps some of them will help you.

Trying Again with a New Baby

Q: I tried to breastfeed my last child (now three), but it lasted only 10 days. I want to try again, but I don't know if I can do it. I was really depressed, cried a lot, and blamed the breastfeeding. Do you think I'll be able to breastfeed my next child?

~ *Lynn, Arkansas*

La Leche League Responds

A: The feelings of depression you describe are common among many postpartum mothers, whether they are breastfeeding or not, especially among those who have had little support from people around them as they were learning this new skill. These feelings are probably caused by hormonal changes, exhaustion from labor and delivery, and the ups and downs that accompany any major life change, such as birth, or new life role, such as motherhood. What we have found in counseling nursing mothers is that breastfeeding makes the hormonal changes after birth occur more gradually. In fact, an Australian study found a lower rate of postpartum depression among breastfeeding women.

Find a support group such as La Leche League in your community [to contact La Leche League, see the Resources section]. It has been our experience that in order to have a satisfying breastfeeding experience, a mother must have accurate information and support. The support should be very practical: for example, getting help for the first one to two weeks so you can focus on your baby and not on cleaning, cooking, or taking care of older siblings. Being able to talk to another nursing mother who can listen to your feelings can help reassure you of the normal course of breastfeeding as well as help you spot any potential problems that may need further attention.

Three Tips for Success

I tried to nurse my son, and it just wouldn't work. He wasn't growing enough and was diagnosed as having a failure to thrive [see Growth] because he just wasn't getting enough milk. When I had my second baby, I was terrified the same thing would happen to her, but we kept at it and suffered through thrush. She ended up nursing almost a year. These are my big three tips for nursing success:

1. If your baby isn't nursing at the hospital, tell the doctor you won't leave until you know that both of you have the hang of it. (This will probably be covered by insurance—believe me, I got a three-day stay out of a 24-hour approved stay from my HMO.) Just explain your concerns.

2. If you have any questions or any concerns, get a referral to an accredited lactation consultant, and make sure she *sees* you, not just coaches you over the phone. If your insurance doesn't cover the service, most lactation consultants will work out payment plans or reduce or even drop the fee if you can't afford it.

3. Buy a nursing pillow. My lactation consultant sold me one called My Breast Friend that uses Velcro and provides some back support. It made it so much easier to work out positioning.
   ~ *Tarrant F., Eugene, Oregon*

Don't Give Up Too Quickly

If you are determined to breastfeed, try every option before you quit.
   ~ *Kristi M., Dallas, Texas*

When It Just Won't Work

I want you all to know that no one can possibly know how hard it can be when you really want to make breastfeeding work and it just won't. I saw lactation consultants; I tried pumping. Then I came to the conclusion that I wasn't seeing my baby because I was constantly hooked up to that darn milking machine, pumping next to nothing. Finally, I made the switch to formula. You have to weigh what's best for you and your baby in the long run, and not just nutritionally. It is hard, though—I know the guilt. Remember that many happy, healthy babies have been bottle-fed.

~ *Parent Soup member Jamie97735*

After I had had a terrible experience trying to breastfeed and had given up, my nurse reminded me that anything that could interfere with my enjoying being a mother could be detrimental to me and my child.

~ *Theresa M., Virginia Beach, Virginia*

Q: I'm trying to nurse my baby, but it's just not working. She cries all the time, and I feel like crying all the time! I really want to quit, but my friends tell me it will hurt my baby's health. I feel overwhelmed. What should I do?

~ *Laurie P., Hoboken, New Jersey*

DR. GREENE'S INSIGHT

A: As a pediatrician I am often asked if either bottle-feeding from birth or weaning from the breast when a baby is very young will negatively affect the baby. This is actually a very difficult question to answer.

The medical facts are that babies and mothers benefit tremendously from the nursing experience and that the baby benefits nutritionally from breast milk. This general truth, however, does not determine whether nursing will be best for a specific mother and baby under their specific conditions.

For some mothers, nursing is either impossible or impractical. Occasionally, nursing can become so stressful that mothers cannot enjoy their babies. I believe that this stress has a profound effect on the child. In addition, if nursing is not going well, it is possible that the baby is not getting adequate nutrition. Alternatively, bottle-fed babies (including many of us who are now parents) grow up healthy and love their mothers.

I recommend that you try a few simple things that might make the situation much easier for both of you before you decide to make the switch, because if you make a hasty switch, you may never be able to go back to nursing:

- Ask the baby's father, a family member, or a close friend to help you for a few days. During that time, pamper yourself!

- Get as much sleep as possible. Let the dirty dishes stack up if you must: there will be lots of time later on for cleaning. Take naps. This is not being lazy; it is being loving.

- Drink at least eight glasses of water a day. This will help increase your milk supply.

- Make sure that baby is sucking and swallowing when at your breast. Don't feed your baby more often than every hour and a half to two hours or your baby may fall into a pattern of nibble nursing. [See Going Back to Work for more information on this topic.]

- You may not feel great about how you look right now. It will take time to get your prepregnancy shape back (although breastfeeding helps most mothers lose weight more quickly). Still, sacrificing proper nutrition in order to lose weight is not in anyone's best interest. Get adequate nutrition and continue taking your prenatal vitamins.

- Talk with your pediatrician or a lactation consultant (or both) who may well have specific insight into your situation.

- Call your obstetrician. You may be suffering from hormonally induced postpartum depression. Help is available.

One of the best things you can do for your daughter's overall health is to keep falling in love with her. If nursing is interfering with this, discontinuing it may be in your daughter's and your family's best interest.

BREASTFEEDING—EXPRESSING MILK
(See also *Going Back to Work*)

You have probably already figured out that breast milk is as valuable as gold. And everyone knows that having a little extra gold tucked away for a rainy day is a good idea. Here are some tips to help you express and store some breast milk so that if you need to be away from your baby, he will still have consistent nourishment.

Pumping

I pumped from 10 weeks to 21 months while working full-time outside the home. I tried to have a minimum of 12 ounces available but sometimes—

depending on my baby's age, growth spurts, and other factors—he would want as much as 20 ounces. We nursed right before I left, as soon as I got home, and throughout the evening and night (no sleeping through for this child!). I recommend making up bottles of no more than four ounces, so none gets wasted until you determine whether your baby ever wants a big feed, like eight ounces. Our son never had more than four ounces in a bottle, although he might have two bottles close together. Another tip—if you are going to be gone for extended periods, I'd say you need a double-electric pump. I never could "grasp" manual expression, though I know it works well for some!

~ *Alisa B., Pelham, Massachusetts*

Storing Breast Milk: Tips from La Leche League

Many parents use disposable plastic bags for storing frozen breast milk. Here are some ideas that have worked for them:

1. If using bags that are not specifically for freezing breast milk, use two in order to prevent breakage.

2. Squeeze out the air at the top and roll down the bag to about an inch above the milk.

3. Close the bag and seal it with a rubber band or twist tie.

4. Note the date it was stored on the bag so you can use the older milk first.

5. Freeze in two- and four-ounce quantities in order to minimize waste and to make thawing easier.

6. Place bags of milk upright in a plastic container (make sure it has a tight-fitting lid) in the freezer in order to safeguard against cross-contamination with other foods.

7. Thaw milk in the bag under cool, then warm, running water. Then snip open the bottom corner with a clean scissors (sterilized if you are saving milk for a sick or premature baby) to drain the milk into a regular feeding bottle or cup.

Also, if you plan to use the milk that you expressed within eight days, you may want to consider refrigeration rather than freezing as your storage method. The antimicrobial qualities of breast milk are preserved when they are not frozen.

BREASTFEEDING—LEAKING
(See also Weaning)

Leaking is a real problem for some women, while others never experience it. It can be triggered by nursing on the opposite side, hearing a baby cry, or simply thinking about your baby! (This must be how men feel when certain parts of their bodies seem to have minds of their own.)

Preventing Leaks: Tips from La Leche League
If you are prone to leaking, you can use a cut-up cloth diaper or commercial pads to keep your outer clothing dry. Be sure the pads are not backed with plastic. With the reusable, cloth type, you can just toss them in the wash with the diapers or baby clothes. When you are out in

public and you begin to leak, hold your forearms across your breasts and press hard. This is relatively unobtrusive and works effectively to stop the leaking. Some women are bothered by heavy leaking at night and wake up in a literally sopping wet bed. Try keeping a handy supply of old, clean towels and cloth diapers. You can fold a towel under the upper half of your body; if the roughness bothers you, place a clean diaper over the towel. If you are bothered by leaking while you are at home nursing, try catching the milk from the opposite breast in a washcloth or diaper. This will save some laundry and save your breast pads for when you are out in public.

Be assured that eventually your body will settle down and the leaking will subside. In fact, some women who leaked heavily while nursing their first baby find they leak much less with subsequent children. The thing to remember is that if you leak, breast milk doesn't stain!

Nighttime Leaks

If you leak at night, try cutting a waterproof sheet or mattress pad to the size of one of your pillowcases. Insert it in the case and put the pillowcase underneath you on top of your mattress. In the morning, you can just toss the case in the dirty clothes and put on another clean one. The waterproof pads are big enough to make more than one leak pad, so you can fix up another one without having to do the wash every day!

~ *Julie, Florida*

Breast Shells

I found that when I nursed, I could have spent more on pads than I would have on formula. Then I found breast shells. For about $6, you can buy shells, which collect the milk you leak, keep you dry, and are reusable. Of course, you discard the milk that collects. They are also great for going back to work. They help keep the milk production going and save with nursing pads.

~ *Patricia, Oregon*

Homemade Nursing Pads

My sister-in-law made her own nursing pads and is making some for me out of cloth diapers. She uses the Sears best-quality diapers that have a layer of sponge in the middle. She just cuts out circles and sews the edges so they don't unravel.

~ *Katie K., Germantown, Wisconsin*

Wait Before You Buy

I wouldn't buy many nursing pads before having a baby. With baby number one, I used one box of them and my supply evened out. With baby number two, I've never needed them and have two extra boxes I bought that are about to become part of a baby gift for someone who's nursing.

~ *Susan W., New York, New York*

BREASTFEEDING—PAINFUL
(Plugged Ducts and Breast Infection)

Breastfeeding, once established with your baby, should not be painful. One major cause of pain while breastfeeding, however, is a plugged milk duct, which can often lead to a breast infection. For information on thrush, another major cause of pain, please see the entry under Thrush.

Home Remedies for Plugged Ducts

I couldn't get any milk out of one breast. I read somewhere to try soaking
the breast in warm water, then try pumping—and *it worked*! I got a full
ounce at the first sitting (before I had only been getting about a quarter
teaspoon), in seven minutes, no less! So now I submerge my breast before
I pump every time. And it helps sore nipples too. I found it to work
better than a hot shower, heating pad, or compresses.

~ *Susan B., Ridgefield, Connecticut*

I suffered from plugged ducts continuously the entire time I breastfed
(eight and a half months). One would clear up, and I would get another.
Here's what helped:

1. A heating pad with a damp washcloth underneath. I did this
   whenever possible.

2. Nursing frequently and *changing positions*. I practically stood on my
   head to try and unclog the lump.

3. Getting plenty of rest. Of course, when you have other little ones, it's
   very difficult but still very important.

~ *Gail T., Mars, Pennsylvania*

Breast Infections

Q: After eight months of nursing, I contracted a breast infection. I have
two questions: Is there anything I can do, besides taking antibiotics,
that will help speed my recovery? How can I avoid getting another
one? I want to keep nursing, but this really hurts!

~ *San Mateo, California*

DR. GREENE'S INSIGHT

A: Breast infections are most common from two to six weeks after birth, but they can happen as long as you are nursing. They are caused by bacteria that normally live on the surface of the breast, and they may be complicated by a clogged milk duct. In many cases the infections are quite painful and can be accompanied by flu-like symptoms. They are nothing to take lightly. Here are some suggestions for speeding your recovery:

- Get lots of rest. Don't wait until you are forced to go to bed—start immediately.

- Drink at least eight glasses of water a day. The kidneys are an incredible filter and help clean the infection out of your system.

- Place moist hot packs on your breasts. This stimulates blood flow to the infected area, which is another way the body has of healing itself.

- Nurse from the infected breast first. You should do this because often the second breast is not fully emptied. Emptying the breast helps speed recovery by keeping fresh milk flowing through the breast. If you do not feel like the breast is empty, pump after each feeding.

- Wear a good nursing bra that fits properly. It should offer support without restricting circulation.

- Transient breast lumps are often present during breast infections. However, if a lump persists, bring it to your doctor's attention.

● Get proper nutrition and continue taking prenatal vitamins. Your overall
health is essential to the healing process.

To minimize the chances of breast infections, follow these general
guidelines just listed and be sure to wash your hands thoroughly before you
touch your breasts. It is easy to go from a diaper change into nursing, but
you must be careful to first wash your hands completely.

No matter how many precautions you take, you may get another breast
infection. The key to minimizing its effect is to treat early and aggressively.
In other words, take good care of yourself.

BOWEL MOVEMENTS *(See Constipation, Diarrhea)*

CHICKENPOX *(See also Immunizations)*

Each year, there are three and a half million cases of
chickenpox in the United States. Dr. Greene explains the
risk that chickenpox poses to babies and how the disease is transmitted.
[For information on the pros and cons of immunizing your baby against
chickenpox, see Immunizations.]

Q: A week ago we were visiting some friends with our eight-and-a-half-
month-old. As we were leaving, they informed us that their oldest boy
had had the chickenpox, that he was no longer contagious, and that
he was returning to school the next day. (Nice of them to wait so long

to tell us! We would never have gone in if I'd known!) What are the chances of my little one getting them? We are waiting and worrying. Is there anything we can do to prevent them? And what should we do if he gets them?

~ *Melinda S., Sherwood, Oregon*

DR. GREENE'S INSIGHT

A: Unfortunately, chickenpox is one of the most contagious childhood illnesses. The disease is usually mild, although serious complications sometimes occur.

People who have chickenpox become contagious 24 hours (and sometimes as long as 48 hours) prior to breaking out. They remain contagious while uncrusted blisters are present, usually one week or less after breaking out. Your little one was only exposed if he was around the infected children either while they had spots or one to two days beforehand. If your son was exposed, he could break out with the chickenpox anytime between 10 and 20 days after the exposure (usually 12 to 16 days).

Children under one year of age whose mothers have had chickenpox are not very likely to catch it. If they do, they often have mild cases because they retain partial immunity from their mothers' blood. Children under one year of age whose mothers have not had chickenpox or whose inborn immunity has already waned can get severe chickenpox.

For children past their first birthday, the chickenpox vaccine can be helpful as prevention, even if it is given after an exposure. In otherwise healthy children younger than one year of age, there is generally nothing that is done to prevent infection.

A safe, effective medicine called acyclovir, or Zovirax, is available if your child does break out with chickenpox. In 1991 a large, well-conducted, multicenter trial of acyclovir therapy for normal children with chickenpox was published in the *New England Journal of Medicine*. Acyclovir was given within 24 hours of the onset of the pox. Children received it four times a day for five days. The children in the treatment group had significantly fewer pox, a shorter duration of forming new pox, reduced itching, earlier healing, and less scarring than the children in the untreated group. There was also a smaller chance of fever, a shorter duration of fever, and an accelerated resolution of all other symptoms in the children treated with acyclovir. If your child breaks out with chickenpox, contact your pediatrician within 24 hours for more information regarding the option of treatment with acyclovir.

Other measures aim at keeping the child comfortable during the infection. Aveeno Bath (or other oatmeal bath) in lukewarm water provides a crusty, comforting coating on the skin. Bathe the child every day and trim the fingernails short to reduce secondary infections and scarring. Benadryl elixir by mouth will help to ease the itching, as will topical lotions such as calamine or Sarna. Most children will recover within the week.

CHILD CARE
(See also Going Back to Work)

A time will come when you are not going to be able to be home with your child. Maybe you need to go back to work, maybe you need to get out of the house for sanity's sake, or maybe you want your child to gain the socialization benefits of day care. Over half of families with parents who can't be home all the time manage to care for their child(ren) without outside help—by either alternating schedules so one parent is always home or relying on relatives. That means half of you who need child care will have to pay someone to take care of your child while you're gone. How do you find someone you can both trust and afford? Here's advice for thinking through your choices and finding the help that's right for you.

Out-of-Home Child-Care Checklist

There are never too many questions to ask when looking for a child-care center for your child. Use this checklist, provided by the Child Care Action Campaign, when conducting your search:

1. **Licensing.** State licensing requirements assure the basic health and safety of a facility in general but may not guarantee the quality you are looking for. Be sure to check your state's licensing standards and ask any prospective care facility if it complies with them. If the child-care facility is not licensed, find out why.

2. **Quality.** Some high-quality, center-based programs have been accredited by the National Association for the Education of Young Children (NAEYC). Ask about a center's accreditation. Even if it has not been accredited, some key elements of quality to look for include staff structure, staff training, interactions between children and providers, cleanliness, safety, and adequate, age-appropriate equipment. Visit the program. Talk to other parents; their experiences can help you learn what to look for.

3. **Group size and ratios.** The most important factors contributing to the quality of a child-care program are group size (the ratio of staff to children) and the staff's training and experience. Studies show that

children benefit the most, both socially and developmentally, from being in smaller child-care groups that allow more direct social interaction between children and caregivers. Although state regulations vary, the following are optimal staff-to-child ratios to ensure that children will receive enough individual attention:

Family day care—One adult to five children, including the caregiver's own (no more than two infants under one year of age).

Day-care centers—One adult to three or four infants or toddlers. Infants should be in a group with fewer than eight children.

4. **Training.** Because there are no consistent standards for child-care staff training, the experience and education of child-care workers vary widely. Qualified staff may have college degrees in early childhood education or a Child Development Associates credential. If the caregivers at a prospective facility do not have such formal training, ask if the program provides in-service training for staff. Firsthand observation is the most reliable means of assessing a caregiver's ability to care for your child. Also ask about staff turnover: low wages for caregivers are the main reason for extremely high turnover in the child-care field, and such turnover negatively affects the quality of care.

5. **Adult-to-child and child-to-child interactions.** Watch carefully to see if the children are busy, happy, and absorbed in their activities. Observe the adults. Are they interested, loving, and actively involved with the children?

6. **Cleanliness.** The spread of infectious diseases can be controlled by cleanliness. Watch to see if teachers or other adults wash their hands

frequently, especially after diaper changing. Are the facilities, toys, and equipment cleaned regularly?

7. Play equipment. A variety of interesting play materials and equipment can help your child achieve physical, social, and intellectual growth. In addition, it's important that each age group be provided with enough age-appropriate play materials. For example, jigsaw puzzles and crayons may be fine for preschoolers but are inappropriate for infants. Keeping this in mind, look for appropriate play materials, such as books, blocks, wheel toys, balls, puzzles, and musical toys.

8. Safety and emergency procedures. There should be an emergency plan clearly posted near the telephone. This should include telephone numbers for a doctor, ambulance, fire department, and police. Smoke detectors should be installed and fire extinguishers must be readily available and in working order. Staff should be trained to deal with emergencies.

9. Price of care. Fees for child-care services vary greatly. The price for family day care ranges from $50 to $120 per child per week. In centers, care for infants (up to two years old) is usually the most expensive, costing between $50 and $200 per week. (In-home caregivers must be paid at least the minimum wage, and parents are responsible for Social Security and other taxes.) Despite the high fees, child-care providers are among the lowest paid in the United States, earning an average of $5.35 per hour. The federal government and some state governments offer tax credit programs to help parents pay for child care; some employers also help out with child-care expenses.

10. Location. Transportation and location, like costs, determine whether a program is within a family's reach. When possible, choose child care close to your home or work. Sometimes a center en route to work, near the school that an older child attends, or near a relative can be a good choice as well.

In-Home Care

If you want to find someone to care for your child in your home, here is a list of steps to take to ensure that you find the right provider, courtesy of the Dependent Care Connection (DCC), a private agency in Westport, Connecticut, that specializes in helping parents find child-care solutions [for more information on the DCC, see the Resources section]:

● Do your homework. Develop a complete, written job description, including specific responsibilities.

● Research your responsibilities when employing in-home help, particularly in the areas of wage and overtime rules, worker's compensation, taxes, U.S. au pair guidelines, if applicable, and so forth.

● Conduct a telephone interview. Inform the candidate of your prerequisites and verify compatibility of schedules, transportation needs, and other practical and legal considerations. Get a general feel for the candidate's character, work habits, motivations, work history, compensation requirements, and suitability for the position.

● Have candidates submit a resume and complete a written application stating general information (name, address, telephone), educational background, work experience, and references.

- Craft interview questions in advance that target the caregiver's beliefs and personality, background and experience, relationships with parents and children, and ability to accommodate special care needs. (Be aware of the appropriateness of your questions and ensure that they fall within your state's employment guidelines.) Develop questions that require both factual and conceptual answers.

- Ideally, schedule at least a one-hour meeting in your home to interview a candidate. Conduct a thorough interview and take note of your first impressions and instincts, as well as the caregiver's body language, answers, and questions.

- Present applicants with a written job description and consider introducing them to your child toward the end of the interview to observe their interaction.

- Call at least three references to gain additional information and insights about prospective caregivers. Develop and write out questions in advance that target the caregiver's history, integrity, personality, and relationships with children and parents. Note any discrepancies between what the caregiver shared during the interview and what the reference states.

- Ask previous employers if they would rehire the candidate and request additional information if the answer is "No." Take notes and listen carefully.

- Conduct a thorough background check of all potential caregivers, either through an in-home agency or by hiring a private investigative firm.

- Background checks should include a full criminal-record search, a driver's record check, and possibly a credit check.

- Avoid extending an offer of employment until you have completed both reference and background checks.

- Keep in mind that no background check is foolproof. Rather, it should be used in conjunction with every tool you have at hand, including interviews, references, friends' advice and experience, agency support, and especially your own best instincts.

- If none of the candidates appear to offer what you are looking for, don't pick the best of the worst. Instead, review your job requirements, make any necessary adjustments, and begin your search again, wiser from the experience.

- Be prepared to commit to a quality search for a caregiver—a search that can take several months to complete.

How to Find Qualified Baby-Sitters

Here is some more information from the Dependent Care Connection on finding a good baby-sitter. It can be done!

You may be surprised by the number of places you can actually search for a part-time caregiver. Your first option is to contact a local in-home or baby-sitting agency for a baby-sitter. Find these listings in the yellow pages under Child Care, through a local resource and referral service, or through your local telephone company's information services. Baby-sitting and in-home agencies draw from a pool of qualified

C   child care

TIPS FROM THE DEPENDENT CARE CONNECTION ON INTRODUCING YOUR CHILD TO DAY CARE

Naturally, young children get attached to their parents, especially their mothers. This attachment can be particularly strong if a child is used to being cared for exclusively by a stay-at-home parent. Very often, separation anxiety can occur when children are cared for by someone other than their parents, especially if care occurs outside their home. Here are some tips for preparing your child to enter a child-care setting for the first time:

• Prepare your child in advance for day care. Practice saying goodbye by leaving your child with a family

candidates to place a caregiver who meets your needs. However, they may require certain application or placement fees, depending on their policies and the hours of care you require. If the sitter you have selected is not a good fit with your family's needs, the agency will usually have others that you can try.

If you prefer to find your own child care, you can post an advertisement, screen applicants, conduct interviews, and perform your own background checks. In your advertisement, be sure to include your name, telephone number, your town, all necessary qualifications, transportation requirements, and other pertinent details regarding your children's care needs. Some viable places to post an advertisement are churches, temples, colleges, high schools, senior or community centers, newspapers, libraries, the Red Cross, YMCAS, and YWCAS. It is not uncommon for caregivers at child-care centers to take on baby-sitting jobs for some extra pocket cash, so you might want to post in these locations as well. Feel free to describe your needs to the caregiver you select and to keep the lines of communication open, should concerns arise.

Finding the Elusive, Quality Baby-Sitter

The Red Cross and the Y in my area both offer baby-sitting courses. They can supply names of graduates who are willing to baby-sit for extra cash. If you've got either of these agencies in your area, give it a call.
~ *Melanie M., Rock Hill, South Carolina*

Day Care—Pre–Potty Training

Q: I am a single mother of a 15-month-old son and am preparing to go back into the workforce, grudgingly. I have heard that most day cares won't take children unless they are potty trained, and as he is still just a little too young to grasp that concept, I am at a loss as to what to do. Any suggestions would be greatly appreciated.

~ *Christina, New York*

A: Yes, it is possible to find good day care for your little one. I have a family day care in my home that I have been running for 20 years now. As you start talking to day-care providers in your area, remember that Mom and provider must work together, so you need to find someone who thinks along the same lines as you do. Ask a lot of questions; the provider shouldn't mind as long as you're patient. And be sure to see how the other kids react to the provider—a sure key to how effective a caregiver is.

~ *Patty, California*

Nannies: Worth the Cost?
In order to find a nanny, my best plan is to network like crazy and just tell everyone you know that you are looking. Once you've found a nanny, the very best thing you can do is to think of the nanny's happiness. If she is good and well qualified for the job and you trust her (I am assuming these all to be true; otherwise why are you leaving your kids with her?), focus on her happiness—and the kids will be happy by default. A great nanny is worth her weight in gold. The worst thing for your kids is to have the transition and inconsistency of switching nannies. Pay as much as you can afford to. Don't look to get a cheap deal, because you'll get what you pay for, and aren't your kids worth it?

~ *Parent Soup member mominluv*

As a caregiver, it has always amazed me that parents have very high expectations (they want you to know first aid, have tons of experience,

member, neighbor, baby-sitter, or friend with whom your child is familiar. Leave your child with these other caregivers for brief periods of time, gradually lengthening the time spent apart.

- If your baby is breast-feeding, use a bottle occasionally and let a friend feed your child. Let others change your child's diapers.

- Gradually introduce your child to outside noises during nap time (i.e., leave a door open or the television or radio on).

- Talk with your child about the new care-givers he or she will have. Show enthu-siasm for the care arrangement with your words and your tone of voice.

43

- Before care begins, introduce your child to the caregiver. Observe their interaction carefully: a good caregiver will understand what your child is feeling and will try to make him or her feel loved and welcome in the new care situation.

- With in-home caregivers, have the new provider perform a task that you are usually in charge of, like preparing your child's snack or changing a diaper. This may help your child warm up to the new caregiver.

- Take your child to visit a new care facility a few days in advance of actual stays there to become familiar with its layout.

cook and clean, keep the TV off, and know all sorts of fun things to do), yet they don't want to *pay* for that. I get paid $10 an hour to clean houses, and half as much to mind children—doesn't make sense to me! Nannies are not in it for the money, that's for sure. But it is sure nice when there are extra little monetary "perks" in the job, like paid holidays or overtime pay. In return, your nanny is helping you raise your children in their home environment, loving them as though they were her own, and giving them security so that they know there are at least three big people in their lives who love and care for them. Children cannot get this same kind of care from day care or a baby-sitter.

~ *Parent Soup member new2this*

Tips from the Dependent Care Connection for Easing the Day-to-Day Transition Between Home and Child Care

Even after your child becomes used to a child-care arrangement, the transition from home to care, even in-home care, can cause minor disturbances on a day-to-day basis. It is important that you help your child ease in and out of a care situation each day. Then, as children get older and attend school, they will be better able to handle these types of transitions on their own.

These are some techniques to ease the daily transition:

- Make sure the staff at the center greets your child warmly and cheerfully on arrival. Take the time to ensure your child gets settled comfortably. This is not the occasion to rush.

- Establish an arrival routine: sign in together, stow belongings, do a short activity together, wave good-bye from a special place.

- Be sure to communicate with the caregiver about your child's activities, moods, and behavior from the morning and the night before. With this information, the caregiver will be better able to respond to your child.

- Have your child bring a favorite toy or other personal item to child care (e.g., a family picture, favorite stuffed animal). The more homelike you can make the care setting, the easier and more enjoyable it will be for your child to go there.

- With in-home care, have the caregiver arrive a short while before you leave for work. Share morning activities with the caregiver, such as preparing breakfast or helping your child dress. This way, your child can become accustomed to the caregiver's presence each morning, and she is likely to be more comfortable by the time you leave.

- Do not leave your child with a caregiver without saying good-bye: if you do this, you risk violating your child's trust.

- Always say good-bye with a kiss, hug, and a wave. Be firm but friendly about leaving. Even if your child whines or clings, a prolonged good-bye will only be harder for both of you.

- Comforting words, such as, "I know it's hard to say good-bye," are helpful. Ridicule, such as "Only babies cry," will not help your child learn to deal with difficult situations. Treat your child with firmness tempered by love and patience.

- On the first day of care, bring a picture of your family for your child to look at during the day.

- As you walk or ride together on that first day, talk or sing. Casually discuss what you will do when you are together again.

- Regularly talk with the child's new caregiver(s) to make sure your child is adjusting well, making friends, and getting involved in daily activities. Most caregivers will automatically provide parents with this type of report, at least during the first few weeks of care.

- Good-byes will be less painful for your child after you have left. If you check with the caregiver, you will probably find that it becomes easier for your child as each day passes.

- Maintain a predictable pickup schedule. Children need to be confident that they can count on you to come back when you said you would.

- When you return at the end of a long day, you and your child may each be running low on energy and patience. You will often have to make a conscious decision to put aside the problems of the day and concentrate on the needs of your child.

- Talk with the caregiver about the day's activities and your child's behavior, moods, and eating and sleeping habits.

- Use commuting time to ease the transition from home to child care and back again. Commuting can be a special time to share accomplishments and ideas, play games, or observe changes in your surroundings. Note: You may want to bring a snack that your child can nibble on during the ride.

- Establish a bedtime ritual to add predictability and continuity to your daily routine.

DR. GREENE'S INSIGHT

Not another ear infection! Kids in day care do get sick more often, but you can keep this to a minimum if the class size is limited to six or fewer. This is especially important during the winter months when your child is younger than two years. You might want to keep the pacifier at home if your child uses one—kids who use a pacifier at day care can get even more ear infections than other kids. [See Pacifiers for more information on this topic.]

CIRCUMCISION

To circumcise or not to circumcise? Not an easy question to answer when custom goes head-to-head with reason. The operation is popular and simple—but painful. The health benefits are controversial. But the procedure has been performed as long as humans have kept records. Ultimately, it's a personal choice. If you've already made the decision, we've added pointers on circumcision and foreskin care. If you haven't decided yet, Dr. Greene elaborates on the pros and cons of circumcision and explains how he handled the quandary with his own sons.

DR. GREENE'S INSIGHT

More than 70 percent of boys in the United States are circumcised these days, making it the most common operation performed on males. (For comparison, the figure for Canada is 48 percent and for the United Kingdom it is 24 percent. Circumcision is uncommon in Europe, Asia, and Central and South America.) In the United States circumcision (like formula feeding and tonsillectomy) reached its peak in the 1950s and 1960s, when about 90 percent of boys were circumcised. During the 1970s, though, circumcision again came into question, and anticircumcision groups sprang up. In 1975 the American Academy of Pediatrics (AAP) boldly declared that there are no valid medical indications for circumcision in the newborn, period.

More recently, new evidence forced the AAP to revise its recommendations. Before we examine the pros and cons, let's consider the newborn's perspective: circumcision hurts! Anesthetics can reduce the pain. A dorsal penile nerve block provides pain control for up to six hours, but it, too, involves a painful injection, prolongs the time the infant is restrained, and can cause complications. More promising is EMLA cream, applied topically an hour before the procedure. Studies have confirmed its efficacy, but its safety has not yet been established, and it has not been approved by the FDA for children under one month of age.

Here is information to consider in favor of circumcision:

- Circumcised males have 10 times fewer urinary tract infections.

- Up to 3 percent of uncircumcised boys will require hospitalization for a kidney infection at some time. In the first months of life, kidney infections can lead to systemic infections and even meningitis. Kidney infections in the first years of life can lead to renal scarring that may progress to end-stage kidney disease in young adulthood. This is the data that most influenced the AAP to revise its stance.

- A lower rate of syphilis, genital herpes, genital warts, and AIDS in circumcised men has been reported in a number of studies. The research also demonstrates a lower rate of transmission of HIV to the partners of circumcised men, independent of other factors. These studies are all retrospective—counting events that have already happened—and thus may not adequately take into account other variables.

- Males circumcised in the newborn period almost never develop cancer of the penis. One study estimates the risk of penile cancer as 1 in 600 uncircumcised males, of whom 25 percent will die of the disease. The rest will have significant consequences.

● Cancer of the cervix has been reported to be less common in the partners of circumcised men. Cervical cancer is much less common in Jewish and Muslim women than in cultures where circumcision is not common. (This evidence, however, is merely circumstantial, and it should still be considered inconclusive.)

● Circumcision usually prevents phimosis—the inability to retract the foreskin at the appropriate age (usually school age). When the foreskin of an uncircumcised penis is first successfully retracted, it sometimes gets stuck. The head of the penis then begins to swell, which often requires an urgent circumcision. Newborn circumcision prevents this uncomfortable emergency, called paraphimosis.

● Circumcision reduces the incidence of balanoposthitis—infection or inflammation of the skin of the penis due to trauma or poor hygiene.

● Effective personal hygiene is easier with a circumcised penis.

● Some boys not circumcised at birth will require the procedure later, at greater cost and greater risk.

On the other hand, here are some facts that seem to favor keeping the natural foreskin:

● The human body comes with an intact foreskin.

- Proper penile hygiene and safe sexual practices will help prevent phimosis, paraphimosis, balanoposthitis, penile cancer, cervical cancer, HIV transmission, and other sexually transmitted diseases. But even in modern times, perhaps this is easier said than done.

- On average, men with an intact foreskin have a longer period of time between erection and ejaculation than their counterparts (but men without foreskins can learn to delay ejaculation).

- Circumcision is painful.

- Circumcision is costly, with more than 140 million health-care dollars spent on the procedure in the United States alone. Some argue, however, that more money would be spent overall if every boy were uncircumcised. I doubt it.

- There are complications of circumcision. The true incidence of complications is unknown, but recent large studies have estimated the risk of complications to be between 0.2 and 0.6 percent. Bleeding is the most common complication, and newborn circumcision should not be performed if there is a family history of bleeding problems. It should also be delayed in any child who is sick or premature or who has any abnormality of the penis.

In light of data like this, the American Academy of Pediatrics revised its earlier anticircumcision stand and in 1988 declared that "newborn circumcision has potential benefits and advantages as well as disadvantages and risks."

To me, the risks and benefits of circumcision are very evenly balanced. Don't be misled by anyone who tells you that one option is clearly better than the other. It comes down to a matter of personal preference. Which advantages are more appealing to you; which disadvantages more problematic? Sometimes it is a question of culture or faith. Sometimes it is a question of fitting in with peers during growing-up years. Sometimes it is a question of beauty, somewhat like pierced ears or noses, shaved legs or underarms. Like a tattoo, circumcision is more permanent (although foreskin reattachment has been done).

I encourage you and your baby's father to follow your hearts. My boys are circumcised, primarily because I am a product of 1950s America, and I wanted to share the circumcision bond with my sons. I now understand that had I waited, they would have been able to make this decision for themselves when they were older.

Circumcision Care

For circumcision, use petroleum jelly (if the hospital didn't send you home with anything) and gauze. Be careful not to use alcohol, because it will sting!

~ Carol N., Rialto, California

Foreskin Care

Q: At my husband's request my 19-month-old son was not circumcised at birth. I am the one who gives him his bath, and mostly I change his diapers every day but never do anything specific to clean his penis. I've heard that I'm supposed to clean it but have no idea what to do, and my husband tells me not to do anything specific. I just want to make sure I'm doing the right thing. Do you have any recommendations?

DR. GREENE'S INSIGHT

A: Today in the office, a great mom asked me about her son's newly acquired habit of licking garden snails. Most little boys have a very different sense of hygiene than their mothers. Therefore, most little boys will not spontaneously wash their hands or clean their penises.

If this conflict weren't enough, sources of child-care information vary widely in their recommendations for care of uncircumcised penises. Some advocate aggressive wiping, using cotton swabs and rubbing alcohol to clean under the foreskin. At the other extreme, some experts suggest doing nothing at all until puberty, saying that the collection of cheesy material under the foreskin is natural and desirable.

First, it's important to understand the structure of the penis. It consists of two main parts, the shaft and the head (which is called the glans). Urine and semen exit the body through a tiny opening at the tip of the glans. At birth, the shaft and the glans are covered by a single continuous layer of skin. In uncircumcised boys, the foreskin at first remains firmly attached to the glans, but gradually over time the attachments are broken (mostly by the stretching resulting from repeated, normal erections). In 90 percent of boys the foreskin is loose and mobile by age two, but the process can sometimes take five or more years. When the foreskin has separated from the glans, the foreskin can easily be retracted, or pulled back, to leave the glans exposed. Throughout life, a cheesy, white material called smegma, consisting primarily of dead skin cells and secretions from sebaceous glands, will accumulate under the foreskin.

In uncircumcised boys, forcibly ripping the foreskin from the glans in the name of hygiene can lead to pain, scarring, and adhesions. Do not try to forcibly retract the foreskin or to clean under it with swabs, antiseptics, or even water. Only the outside of the foreskin needs to be cleaned during the first year. Just like the rest of the diaper area, it should be cleaned and bathed with soap and water. After your son's first birthday, you might want to pull back very gently on the skin of the shaft to see if the foreskin retracts. If it doesn't at all, don't worry—and don't force it! As long as the

foreskin doesn't easily retract (even in a 10-year-old), only the outside
needs to be washed. If the foreskin retracts a little, it would be OK to
gently clean the exposed part of the glans with water (but don't use soap
while the foreskin is still partially attached to the glans, because this can
irritate this tender area). After cleaning, always pull the foreskin forward to
its usual position. This is very important: otherwise, it can get stuck and
lead to problems.

Once the foreskin has completely separated and retracts freely, begin
to teach your son to retract his own foreskin and clean underneath it when
he bathes or at least once a week. For most little boys this personal
cleaning will not become a habit unless you encourage it. Mentioning it

PARENT POLL

Did you/would you have your son circumcised?

Of 3,233 total votes

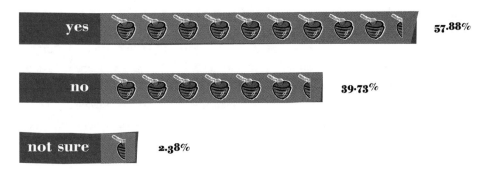

yes — 57.88%

no — 39.73%

not sure — 2.38%

1 bowl = 200 parents

positively and frequently throughout the years can instill an important sense of responsibility, prevention, and health that will benefit him for years to come. In fact, it's been suggested that proper personal hygiene can help reduce sexually transmitted diseases and cancer of the penis (and cervix in his partner) when your little boy becomes a man.

The best thing for loosening foreskin is to let your child do it himself. Let him run around bottomless part of the day; boys being boys, he will pull at it and such until it retracts just fine. My son would pull his so that it looked like he was pulling taffy. I was sure he was going to hurt himself, but his doctor said that all was fine and a much safer and natural way to go about it. By the way, have you seen how far a foreskin is supposed to retract? It isn't as far as you think.

~ *Tarrant F., Eugene, Oregon*

COLDS *(See also Croup)*

Of course, there's no cure for the common cold. But you can do things to relieve your baby's symptoms (imagine being stuffed up without being able to even blow your own nose!). And after Parent Soup parents share their ideas, Dr. Greene provides some insight on smart ways to minimize your child's risk of becoming infected with a cold virus.

Clearing Congestion

Try a drop or two of nasal saline to thin out the mucus so it drains more easily. The humidifier is a great idea, and I don't think you can run one too often, especially in cold climates where home heating systems dry out the air. Also, it might help to elevate the head end of the crib, so baby isn't lying flat. If you are formula-feeding, you might want to talk to your pediatrician about the possibility of your baby's being allergic to it. My son seemed to have a constant cold, and I always thought he would grow out of it. Turns out that he was allergic to milk—the milk-based formula we fed him was the culprit.

~ *Lisa K., Tucker, Georgia*

I put my baby in his bouncy chair in the bathroom with me while I take a hot shower. The steam from the shower clears his nose, and when I am done, I use a bulb syringe (what I call his nose sucker) and suck out all the bad stuff that the steam has brought to the surface.

~ *Teleasa, Maryland*

Be gentle with the bulb syringe—you should remove only what you can see in the nose.

~ *Susan H., Syracuse, New York*

When your baby has a cold, dab Vasoline on the tissue before you wipe her nose. This will prevent chafing her already tender skin.

~ *Ann Marie M., Lincoln University, Pennsylvania*

Avoiding Medicine
I don't give a cold remedy at all unless there's a cough or fever involved. I believe that if you let a cold run its natural course, it will clear up faster. When my daughter has a cold, I put on the humidifier and use saline drops. The cold usually lasts only three to four days.

~ *Carla, Maryland*

When to Call the Doctor

Unless you think something is wrong with your child that you can't handle at home, you might want to avoid the doctor's office during the winter if at all possible. Even though we kept my son isolated from other patients and didn't let him touch anything, he picked up a virus there this winter and last winter. The only time he got sick was after a doctor's appointment.

~ Suzanne L., Pasadena, California

Antibiotics for the Common Cold?

Q: Are antibiotics appropriate therapy for the common cold?

~ Emilie O., San Francisco, California

DR. GREENE'S INSIGHT

A: There are more than one billion colds in the United States annually, with each child averaging three to eight colds per year. Two things you should know are that *viruses* cause colds, and that antibiotics kill *bacteria*. Most people mentally lump together viruses and bacteria, but they are entirely different entities.

Viruses are tiny structures that can only reproduce inside a living cell. Outside a living cell a virus is dormant, but once inside it takes over the resources of the host cell and begins the production of more virus particles. They are more like mechanized bits of information, or robots, than like animal life. Bacteria, on the other hand, are one-celled living organisms. If a bacterium were the size of a human, a typical virus particle would be the size of a mouse. Although bacteria can cause disease in humans, many are also quite beneficial.

Antibiotics do not work at all in treating the common cold. Antibiotics kill bacteria, not viruses. A net designed to trap a human might allow a tiny mouse to escape. In fact, antibiotics can actually make colds worse: they can indiscriminately kill the beneficial bacteria; possibly cause diarrhea, yeast infections, and bacterial superinfections; and create an environment more hospitable to cold viruses.

If the one billion colds in the United States this year were "treated" with antibiotics, billions of dollars would be spent, at least 100 million people would suffer adverse side effects, and *zero* people would end their cold more quickly or even have milder symptoms.

CONGESTION *(See Colds)*

CONSTIPATION

Parents are always fascinated by their baby's bowel movements. It really is incredible that such a small creature can have such a high output of waste. But when that output decreases, parental anxiety rises. To help set your mind at ease and your baby's bowels in motion, here are some homegrown remedies. Dr. Greene then offers a good explanation of possible causes and treatments of constipation.

Natural Remedy

Maltsupex is an all-natural remedy for constipation. [Dr. Greene also has an all-natural remedy—see his suggestion in the response that follows.] Ask your local pharmacy if they carry it, or check your local health food store. It's a liquid and pretty expensive, but it has a 10-year shelf life. You can add it in the baby's bottle or cup, whether it's juice, milk, or whatever.

~ *Janet H., Havertown, Pennsylvania*

C constipation

Just What Is Regularity?

From what I've read, heard, and experienced, a bowel movement every three days (particularly in a breastfed baby) until she starts solids is nothing to worry about as long as the stools are soft. Don't worry; your baby will make up for it later!

~ *Julie K., Powder Springs, Georgia*

Easy Ways to Treat Your Child

Sometimes when my son suffers from constipation, I have put prune juice in his Rice Pablum and he never suspects anything. Another thing that helps is chocolate, used with caution (because of the caffeine). I give my son a couple of M&M's every day and it helps.

~ *Ehatch1201*

> **DR. GREENE'S INSIGHT:** Yum! But you might not want to get kids used to sweets so young. Also, because of the caffeine, this is appropriate only for babies older than six months.

Is Three Days Between Stools OK?

Q: My seven-week-old son hasn't pooped in three days. All he gets is breast milk. Is this normal? Is he constipated? If he is constipated, what should I do?

~ *Maria M., Brooklyn, New York*

DR. GREENE'S INSIGHT

A: During your baby's first year, his stools will undergo several changes. The first poops are the thick, sticky, tarry meconium stools that consist partly of old skin cells shed and then swallowed while the baby is still inside the womb. These stools only last a week. Then, the stools will change according to what your baby eats. Here are some details.

Breastfed babies have soft, yellow stools that look like yellow mustard with little seeds. As stools go, they are relatively pleasant and not too smelly. By the time a baby is one week old, he has an average of eight to ten of these stools each day. This number drops to about four per day by four weeks old, and by eight weeks many breastfed babies often go less than once a day. I know many babies who only go every three days.

Formula-fed babies usually stool less often than their breastfed counterparts, and the stools do not change much with time until solid foods are introduced. Formula-fed stools are often tan or yellow and a little firmer than breast-milk stools. For any baby, tan, yellow, green, or brown stools can all be normal. By eight weeks old the formula-fed baby's average drops to one stool per day.

What Is Too Long Between Stools?

If a happy, formula-fed baby goes four days or a breastfed baby goes seven days without a stool, I recommend that he or she be checked by a pediatrician (sooner if the child seems to be in pain). Still, it can be completely normal to go only once every eight days—as long as the stool is soft when it comes out. Stools that are hard (firmer than peanut butter) or foul smelling (you'll know) in a child who has not yet had solid foods may represent something as simple as needing more to drink (especially during hot weather), but they may also be the sign of constipation. Contact your pediatrician to discuss the situation. Also contact your pediatrician if the baby is less than a month old and hasn't gone for four days.

Remedies

With infants, one teaspoon of light Karo syrup in four ounces of water will often get things back on track. When kids begin to eat baby food, the stools change once again. They may be either softer or firmer, but they will likely smell worse (kids also smile and laugh more at this age, more than making up for the unpleasantness). Most children's intestines are very

responsive to the foods they eat. Bananas,
rice cereal, and applesauce all tend to
produce firmer stools. Carrots and squash
are constipating for some babies. Pears,
peaches, plums, apricots, peas, and
prunes make stools softer. By balancing the
diet, you can often keep the stools
comfortably midrange. If the stools are still

too firm, juice is the gentlest medicine to soften them up. Apple juice twice
a day usually works well, but if it doesn't, prune juice is even better. Also,
when your baby is straining, you might want to put him in a tub of warm
water. This will relax his muscles and make the stool easier to pass.

Glycerin suppositories can be very helpful if diet and juice don't work,
but constipation that is stubborn enough to make these optimal should be
discussed with your pediatrician. The same holds true for baby laxatives
(*hint*: if your pediatrician does recommend a laxative, one-half teaspoon of
unprocessed bran mixed with food twice a day is cheaper than Maltsupex
and about as effective).

COUGHING (See Croup)

CRADLE CAP

Cradle cap is scaly skin on your baby's scalp. It can make
your baby look like a reptile, albeit an adorable one, but don't
panic! As Dr. Greene explains, it's a good thing:

DR. GREENE'S INSIGHT

Cradle cap is very common in infants. It is a sign of healthy skin growth, so if your child has it, consider yourself (and your beautiful baby) lucky! Here's how it works: we are constantly making new skin cells at about the rate that we lose old, dry skin cells. The old skin falls off and we usually don't even notice the process. In healthy infants, the skin cells on their scalp are growing faster than they fall off, leaving a layer of extra, somewhat crusty skin. If it isn't bothering baby (sometimes it itches), you don't need to do anything about it. But if it is bothering your infant or you, there is no problem with gently removing it. Simply rub a small amount of baby oil or olive oil onto your baby's scalp. Wait a few minutes for it to soften, and brush it away with a soft brush or a dry terry-cloth washcloth. The oil will leave baby's hair a bit limp, so you may want to do this right before bath time.

In serious cases or if your baby is older than six months, you can apply a small amount of hydrocortisone cream to the scalp or wash the baby's hair with Neutrogena T-Gel shampoo. T-Gel is an adult shampoo and doesn't have the "no tears" factor, so be careful not to get any in your child's eyes.

Other Ways to Get Rid of Cradle Cap

My son had cradle cap for quite a while, and the prescription shampoo my pediatrician gave me didn't help much. What I finally learned from other mothers was to brush his hair with a soft brush every day and then shampoo it. It worked within a week.

~ *Tracey B., Woodhaven, New York*

My doctor told me to use Selsun Blue on my daughter's cradle cap. It cleared it right up!

~ *Parent Soup member Honeypup*

My home nurse recommended that I buy the softest toothbrush available, put shampoo on the bristles, and brush the baby's scalp with it during the bath. I did it from my son's first bath, and he absolutely loved it! And he never had cradle cap.

~ *Missy S., Edgewood, Maryland*

CRAWLING

It's so tempting to push our little ones to the next level of development. After all, one part of a parent's job is to help teach your children. When it comes to crawling, keep in mind that once babies become mobile, your life will never again be the same. Ever. So take a little bit more time to appreciate your baby who can't move around yet without your help. Soon enough you'll be chasing her around, wondering how such a small creature can have so much energy.

When Should a Baby Start Crawling?

Q: My seven-and-a-half-month-old grandson isn't crawling yet. Although he sits alone, he doesn't seem interested in moving around on his stomach. My daughter has tried to show him how to crawl by moving his arms and legs, but he just gets upset. Any advice?

~ *Alberta L. R., Farmington, Connecticut*

DR. GREENE'S INSIGHT

A: We have just recently begun to understand the process of normal child development. It's exciting to know what to expect at different stages and to be able to relate to children more appropriately. One downside of this

62

newfound knowledge is the increased tendency to compare children, both with each other and with the "average ages" for attaining developmental milestones. We feel proud when a child is ahead of his peers and are concerned when he seems to lag behind. But in reality, standardized development charts and tables are nothing more than averages. Each individual child develops and blossoms in his own way and at his own pace.

This is our goal: to provide a nurturing environment where a child can develop at his optimum pace. We don't want to hurry him; we do want to encourage him. We also want to identify anything that may be an obstacle in his path.

Rolling over, sitting without support, cruising (walking along furniture), and walking independently are important developmental milestones. Crawling isn't. Crawling isn't even mentioned in my favorite pediatric-development textbook.

This seems strange since crawling is associated with babies. The truth is that many babies never crawl! They do need to find some way to move across the floor. Each will do so at unpredictable times and in distinctive ways. Your grandson may be a scooter, one who likes to stay upright and scoot across the floor on his bottom. Many babies prefer creeping, or wriggling forward on the stomach. Many children will crab-crawl, moving backward. And, of course, many children will get up on all fours and crawl forward in the traditional way. Each child is unique.

Some adults are concerned that children who don't crawl in the traditional way will be less coordinated. This is a myth. As long as the baby begins to move across the floor using each arm and each leg, there is no cause for concern.

I'm reluctant to mention time frames, but at sometime between six and ten months I expect babies to discover some way to move horizontally across the floor to get desired objects. Obstacles to this include the child's not spending enough time on the floor, using an infant walker (which often eliminates the desire to learn crawling behaviors—infant walkers are bad for proper development [see Toys]), having toys brought to him, being pushed to learn to crawl, and having physical problems, such as muscle weakness. If babies actually crawl, it usually begins at about eight to ten months.

Crawling may be encouraged by spending time on the floor with the baby, placing favorite toys just out of reach, putting a dog-bone pillow or a rolled towel under his chest when he's on his stomach to keep his head up so he can look around and enjoy himself more, and putting a hand behind his feet to give him something to push against if he tries to crawl.

PARENT POLL

How old was your child when she started crawling?

Of 638 total votes

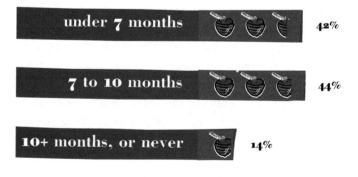

under 7 months — 42%

7 to 10 months — 44%

10+ months, or never — 14%

1 bowl = 100 parents

Observe your grandson's spontaneous play. This will give you the best clues to the developmental tasks that are important for him to learn next. Children tend to be most excited about skills they are on the brink of mastering. If you try to engage him in an activity that is beneath his developmental level, he will quickly get bored. If you try to interest him in something that he is not yet ready for, he will become upset. Our task is to find that zone of moderate challenge—where learning is fun. Provide situations where he can teach himself through playful exploration. Forced teaching hinders development.

Don't push him; don't force him on his stomach if he's unhappy; don't try to get him to move his arms and legs. Relax. Enjoy him. Remove any obstacles to crawling that you can identify. Gently encourage him. And sit back and marvel as the inner drive to grow propels him forward.

CROUP

Picture this scene: you're spending a quiet evening at home with your one-year-old son, who has a touch of a cold. At about 8 o'clock he begins coughing—a really loud cough that you can hear throughout the house. It only gets worse over the next few hours. He gets a fever. At 11 o'clock (when all the after-hours clinics have closed and his doctor is in bed), his breathing becomes noisy and labored. Each breath now makes a strange crowing noise that you've never heard before. Concerned, you bundle him up and take him to the local emergency room. As you pull into the ER driveway, you notice that your child seems much, much better. After some heated debate with yourself or your partner (during which the little boy falls asleep peacefully), you decide to head home without being seen. An hour later, at home, his cough comes back, he wakes up, and his breathing is even more difficult. If this scenario sounds familiar, what you were probably experiencing was a case of croup. Dr. Greene explains how to recognize and treat croup:

DR. GREENE'S INSIGHT

The child described in the scenario has a classic case of croup. Croup tends to happen in children between three months and five years old. It is characterized by a brassy cough that sounds somewhat like a seal barking. The word *croup* comes from an old Germanic word for the voice box. Croup, or laryngotracheo-bronchitis, refers to swelling centered at the larynx or vocal cords. It can be caused by infection, allergy, or a foreign body. Most children have what appears to be a mild cold for several days before the barking cough becomes evident some evening. As the cough gets more frequent, the child may start making a harsh, crowing noise as he breathes. Croup typically worsens at night. It often lasts five or six nights, but the first night or two are usually the most severe.

How to Treat It

As the parents in the opening scenario discovered after they made the drive to the hospital, cool night air can briefly decrease the swelling in the larynx and improve the symptoms. Home treatment usually consists of a misting treatment. A cool-air nebulizer is best, but if that is unavailable, the steam from a shower or bath in a closed bathroom can be used. Acetaminophen [Tylenol] can make the child more comfortable and lower any fever. Avoid cough medicines, unless you discuss them first with your doctor. Most cases of croup can be safely managed at home.

I would recommend at least talking with your health-care provider by phone about any case of croup, to let her or him listen to the child's breath and cough. If the child has the crowing noise constantly, he should be seen immediately. If you suspect a foreign body or an insect sting as the cause of croup, he should be seen immediately. He should also be seen immediately if his ribs tug in as he breathes, if he is drooling or very agitated, or if he has dusky lips. Armed with understanding instead of feeling panicked and confused, you can view those long croup nights as occasions for loving and watchfulness.

CRYING AND COLIC *(See also Spoiling)*

Crying is the only way babies can communicate wants and needs. Their crying can mean "I'm wet," "I'm hungry," "I'm tired," or "I want to play." As your baby gets older, you'll start to understand how different cries mean different things. But the overwhelming message that comes across when a baby cries is, "I need attention." And when your baby is crying and nothing you do seems to console her, well, there's no more frustrating feeling in the world (not to mention the strain it causes on your ears!). As Parent Soup member Bonnie G. puts it, "Crying is just so hard to deal with because it renders us adults helpless. Sometimes all that can be done is to grin and bear it." Easily said, but when your baby has been screaming for the past two hours and you don't know what to do, these words of wisdom are little consolation.

When crying lasts longer than three hours a day, it is defined as colic. However, as Dr. Greene says, almost all children will develop a fussy period. And even if the wailing doesn't qualify as colic, these crying stretches can wreak havoc on your sanity. Will you spoil the baby if you run and pick her up whenever she cries? Will she soothe herself much faster if you let her cry it out? Different tactics work for different babies. When we polled Parent Soup parents, 47 percent said that cuddling and rocking were the best ways to calm their babies down. But 23 percent said that something different worked each time. Because what works one time may not work another time, here's a variety of solutions. Keep in mind that you are learning how to best interact with your child, and your child is learning that her parents will take care of her no matter how loud she wails.

Diversionary Tactics

When my three-month-old gets irritable, I take her to the mirror. I carry her, my lunch, and the cordless phone to our full-length mirror and sit Indian style right in front of it. She smiles and is in awe of the other baby staring back at her. Usually, she forgets all about being upset.

~ *Tiffany C., Hawthorne, California*

Contact = Comfort

One of the sure ways of dealing with colic is to get a sling and carry your baby for much of the day. Babies just want to be held right next to their mothers' warm bodies.

~ *Yolanda D., Wausau, Wisconsin*

Fussy babies are often soothed by skin-to-skin contact. Make sure the room is warm, then take off your clothes as well as hers and rock her. This close, secure feeling can help her relax.

~ *Noni B., Lafayette, Louisiana*

Infant massage may soothe a high-need, colicky baby. Look into learning this technique. Contact the International Association of Infant Massage at (800) 248-5432 to learn more.

~ *Ann Marie M., Lincoln University, Pennsylvania*

The Old Put-the-Baby-on-the-Dryer Trick

Our son found instant relief from colic from the oddest of sources. Same time every evening when he would begin to cry, we would place him in his infant seat and put him on top of the clothes dryer, fluff, no heat. We would stand right next to him, and in minutes, not only did he stop crying, but he fell asleep. Every time!

~ *Renee C., Fayetteville, Arkansas*

Hey, It Worked for Someone Else!

My husband and I stumbled on a trick that works like magic when our baby is crying. We chant the vowels. We occasionally vary the pitch and melody, but, regardless, it nevers fails! Sometimes she is screaming her head off, and as soon as we start a-e- . . . she shuts up and smiles. (Of course, we may look a little silly chanting our vowel song in public places, but we think it's better than a screaming baby.)

~ *C. Sturm, Missouri*

Going Up?

The one trick that has never failed me is the elevator move: pick your baby up and hold her close and move up and down, bending at the knees, like a half squat. Move and see how she likes it. It worked every time for us and still does. It's pretty good exercise, too.

~ *Parent Soup member carly'smom*

C crying and colic

If at First You Don't Succeed. . . .

Try every remedy you can think of—walking with the baby, placing warm towels on her tummy, running the vacuum or dishwasher. Sometimes something will work, the next time it won't. So get a good repertoire and keep trying until something helps!

~ *Tamara P., Toronto, Ontario*

Crying It Out vs. Consoling

I have three children—a son and twin girls. I never let my son cry out any of his crying fits. I tried holding him with a warm hot-water bottle, putting a warm receiving blanket in his crib for him to lie on, going for walks—you name it. He was twice as fussy and cranky as my girls. When they would cry, I'd set a timer and check on them every 15 minutes. Until the timer went off, I'd watch TV in another room, go in the bathroom and turn on the fan, or read a book. I learned to wait 20 minutes before going in to check on them, and they would be asleep. It cut the whole crying process at least in half.

~ *Cindy J., Eugene, Oregon*

Take a Break

When all else has failed, try putting baby down in another room. Then put some soothing music in the CD player and close your eyes and ears. Give yourself a break.

~ *Bonnie G., Tewksbury, Massachusetts*

If Breastfeeding, Look to Your Diet for Triggers

Q: My baby starts to scream after some feedings but not after others. We are sure that pepperoni pizza did not agree with him. I have heard spicy foods and dairy products can be a problem as well. What other foods can cause problems? How do I go about finding out what is bothering him? How soon after I eat something that bothers him will it start to affect him, and how long before it doesn't anymore?

~ *Melanie L., Raleigh, North Carolina*

La Leche League Responds

A: Many babies have fussy periods in the first few months, and it can be a challenge to figure out what causes them. Dairy products are one of the most common sources of food sensitivity. A simple way to check whether this is causing your baby's problem is for you to eliminate milk products from your diet for ten days to two weeks and observe your baby to see whether the fussy periods improve. Sometimes, simply eliminating milk, cheese, and ice cream from the mother's diet will make a big difference.

Another way for you to see if your baby's fussiness is caused by foods you are eating is to keep a food diary and note what you eat and drink and when your baby is fussy. Keep in mind that babies can also be sensitive to supplemental vitamins, caffeine, and nicotine as well as to foods. Is there a family history of food sensitivities or allergies? With some trial and error and a bit of luck, you may be able to minimize your baby's fussiness.

DR. GREENE'S INSIGHT

Almost all babies develop a fussy period. The timing varies, but it usually begins at about three weeks of age and peaks somewhere between four and six weeks of age. When the crying lasts for longer than three hours a day, it is called colic, and the phenomenon is present in almost all babies—only the degree is

C crying and colic

TRIVIA QUESTION

Studies show that having this in the home will increase the likelihood of colic:

a. Older sibling

b. Indoor plants

c. Pets

d. Smokers

e. Cable television

Answer: d

The screaming fits seem to be exacerbated by the presence of cigarette smoke.

different. What's important is not whether your baby has colic, but how you deal with the crying. Crying spells can be some of the most frustrating experiences of your life. If you look at them as learning experiences, however, rather than evidence of a medical problem, you will be able to deal with them better.

Why Colic Is Good for You and Your Baby

I believe that colic exists to bring about an important rite of passage within families. *Colic demands attention.* As parents grope for ways to ease their child's crying, they come to grips with the fact that babies are individuals with needs. Parents instinctively pay more attention, talk to the child more, hold the child more, all because of colic.

Helping a child with colic is primarily a matter of experimentation and observation. Different children are comforted by different measures. The process involves trying many things and paying attention to what seems to help, even if it's just a little bit.

- Holding your baby is the most effective way to curb colic. The more hours babies are held, even when they aren't fussy, the less time they will cry in the evening. Do not worry about spoiling your child!

- Lullabies can be powerfully soothing to babies. There's a reason almost every culture has developed some sort of lullabies. [See pages 224–225 for some original lullaby ideas.]

- As babies cry they swallow air, creating gas and abdominal pain and causing more crying. It's a difficult cycle to break. Gentle rocking is comforting and helps babies pass gas. When you get tired, an infant swing is a good alternative for babies at least three weeks old with good head control.

From *Parent Soup: The Game*

Holding your baby in an upright position or placing a warm towel or hot-water bottle on the baby's stomach can also help relieve gas. Some parents report an improvement after giving simethicone drops, a defoaming agent that reduces intestinal gas. It is not absorbed into the body and is quite safe. If nothing else seems to work, try taking your baby's rectal temperature. This will help babies pass gas. [See also Gas.]

PARENT POLL

When your baby would cry for hours on end, what soothing method worked best for you?

Of **1,385** total votes

crying it out 10.83%

cuddling and rocking  47.43%

wearing baby in a sling  19.06%

something different every time  22.67%

1 bowl = 100 parents

- If you're breastfeeding, the foods you eat can affect your baby's colic. Stimulants such as caffeine (including the caffeine found in chocolate) should be avoided. Conversely, a single glass of wine may help you and baby relax. The other foods in mom's diet that are most likely to cause a problem are dairy products and nuts. Try eliminating them for a few weeks. Again, it's a matter of experimentation and observation.

- Even though dealing with colic is an exercise in family bonding, taking a break is also a good idea. You will be able to pay more loving attention to your baby when you've had a chance to refresh yourself.

The most important thing to remember is that colic will not last forever! After about 6 weeks of age it begins improving, slowly but surely, and is usually gone by 12 weeks of age. In the meantime, keep trying different things and paying attention to your baby's responses. As you work together, lasting, new depths will be forged in your relationship.

DIAPER RASH

Diapers may be a lifesaver for parents and babies alike, but they are also the frequent and generous hosts to bacteria, often resulting in a diaper rash. One solution is to let your child go without a diaper for a while, but obviously this is not a long-term solution. Here, Dr. Greene outlines the various types of diaper rash, and Parent Soupers share their tips for beating rashes.

DR. GREENE'S INSIGHT

Diaper rash is the most common skin disorder of infancy. A surprising number of different entities are called diaper rash:

- Friction rash is the most common form of diaper rash, and it affects almost all babies at some time. It is most common on areas where friction is most pronounced, such as the inner thighs or under elastic diapers that are too tight. It comes and goes quickly and responds well to frequent diaper changes, airing out, and protective barriers.

- Irritant rash is most conspicuous on the exposed areas, such as the round part of the buttocks. It tends to spare skin folds and creases. It's generally the result of contact with stool enzymes or irritants, such as harsh soaps, baby wipes, detergents, or topical medicines.

- Allergic rash may occur in combination with an irritant rash or by itself. It, too, is more common on exposed areas and looks like the rash caused by poison oak.

- Intertrigo is a common type of diaper rash caused by moist heat. Occurring deep in the skin folds, the rash-involved skin looks thin, as if it has lost several layers.

- Seborrhea rash is a salmon-colored, greasy rash characterized by yellowish scales. This diaper rash is also worse in the skin folds.

- Psoriasis is a stubborn rash that doesn't necessarily look distinctive. Other signs of psoriasis usually accompany the diaper rash, though, such as pitting of the nails or dark red areas with sharp borders and fine silvery scales on the trunk, face, or scalp.

- **Yeast** is by far the most common type of organism found in a diaper rash. The organism is quite prevalent and thrives on warm, moist skin. Yeast involvement should be suspected in any diaper rash that has not improved dramatically with 72 hours of appropriate therapy. Current or recent antibiotic use makes a yeast infection even more likely, because the medication reduces the amount of the skin's "good" bacteria that fight infection. Classically, a yeast rash is beefy red with sharp, raised borders and white scales. Small satellite lesions surround the main rash. Even without the classic pattern, however, yeast is often present. If you suspect your child has a yeast rash, try adding a cream such as Lotrimin AF to your usual diaper-rash regimen. Continue air drying and applying a protective layer, such as Desitin, over the Lotrimin. Washing with warm water may also be helpful. If the rash has not improved within 72 hours with this treatment, it is probably still a yeast infection, but contact your doctor for additional help.

Homemade Diaper Rash Help

One thing that has all but eliminated diaper rash in my house is homemade diaper wipes. Cut soft paper towels in half and fold them in thirds so that they'll fit in the wipe container. Mix one cup of water, one tablespoon of baby wash, and one tablespoon of baby oil. Not only does the homemade version help with diaper rash, but instead of paying $3 for a container of wipes, I'm now paying about 60¢!

~ *Deborah H., Gary, Tennessee*

Double-Pronged Approach
We use Maalox and Desitin mixed together. It really works! I put it on the
baby's bottom at night, and the next morning the rash is almost
completely gone.
  ~ *Nancy E., New York, New York*

What to Do When the Pharmacy's Closed
I have been down the diaper-rash road many times with my daughter.
Hydrocortisone 2.5% is the best solution we've found, but it requires a
prescription. What I do during the weekend or off-hours is buy zinc
oxide. It's sold over-the-counter, works great, costs only about $1 a tube,
and is very thick. Urine and feces can't penetrate it.
  ~ *Susan N., Fairhope, Alabama*

Soothing the Pain
When baby has a diaper rash, don't use wipes on her bottom. Instead,
wash her with plain water and dry with a blow-dryer set on cool air.
She'll love it!
  ~ *Noni B., Lafayette, Louisiana*

DIAPERS

Cloth or disposable, the earth or convenience, cheap or
expensive—the arguments can go on and on. We're not going
to preach that you should use only cotton diapers. But we have included
some strong arguments for cloth, as well as instructions for washing
them, should you not have access to a good diaper service. Actually,

d diapers

TEN WAYS
TO MAKE
IT UP TO
MOTHER EARTH

1. Shake all poop out of disposable diapers before you throw them away. This reduces the solid waste and the amount of space the diaper will take up in the landfill.

2. Use diaper liners. If the liner gets wet, that is all that needs to be replaced. You'll go through only three or four diapers per day, instead of six to nine.

3. Stop using disposable grocery bags. Buy a sturdy canvas bag and keep it in

most parents on our boards use a combination of diapers: cloth during the day and disposable at night or for travel. Of course, there are good reasons to use disposables (e.g., you don't have access to a diaper service or a washing machine, your septic system can't handle all the laundry, or you don't even have time to wash your hair much less loads of diapers). Just remember that every diaper takes nearly five hundred years to decompose. So if you use disposable diapers, read the sidebar about 10 ways to make it up to Mother Earth.

First, let's consider **cloth diapers**.

Some Benefits of Cloth

My daughter lets me know when she needs to be changed much more quickly in a cloth diaper than in a disposable one.

~ *Sara S., Eugene, Oregon*

My daughter has very sensitive skin, but she has not had one diaper rash with the cloth diapers. Thank God!

~ *Chantel A., Auburn, Washington*

Washing Diapers at Home

I wash our cotton diapers since our diaper service went out of business (sad!). Here's how:

1. I don't soak them in the diaper pail but just shake out BMs into the toilet.

2. On wash day, I prewash in warm water with a small amount of regular detergent. (You can skip this step, but I think it gets the diapers cleaner.)

3. Soak (overnight if you can, but a few hours is OK) in warm water with a cup of weak hydrogen peroxide solution (half to one ounce of hydrogen peroxide to one cup of water).

4. Use the regular wash cycle with hot water.

5. Every so often, do a second rinse with vinegar in the wash water.

This may look burdensome, but I've been doing diapers once a week for about six months. I have four dozen diapers and use disposables at night (cheaper than doing the bedclothes every day). For an infant, you may go through diapers faster and either will need more diapers or will need to wash twice a week. You can always fold diapers to fit, so buying infant-sized ones aren't necessary. It's really not a bother at all, and it saves us a ton of money. I wish I'd done it with our first!
~ *Lisa C., Newton, Massachusetts*

Now, for a look at the alternative, let's consider **disposables**.

Finding a Disposable Diaper That Works
Cloth diapers were not an option for us, and I found the best way to find a diaper was to buy some small packages of a few different kinds to figure out which ones we liked.
~ *Mary L., Dover, Pennsylvania*

Money-Saving Tips
1. Skip the newborn size and purchase the small size instead. You get twice as many diapers for the same price. To avoid cord stump irritation, fold the diaper back at the waist.

your car—it will hold more groceries and make them easier to carry. Best of all, you'll be teaching your kids about reusing instead of just recycling.

4. Stock up on baby supplies. To avoid extra trips to the store in your car, try to consolidate excursions or run those errands on foot to cut down on gasoline consumption.

5. Plant a tree in honor of your child's birthday. Not only will the tree provide shade and oxygen (while absorbing carbon dioxide), but you can take a

picture of your child in front of it every year as documentation of how much he's growing.

6. Don't buy toys that require batteries. They tend to end up on the shelf after their novelty has worn off. Try toys that run on imagination, such as books, puppets, and stuffed animals.

7. Buy organic. If pesticide-free produce isn't available, talk to your grocer. Not only will it keep your family healthier, it will reduce chemical runoff in our water systems.

2. Call the diaper manufacturers and ask to be put on their coupon list. Here are the numbers for the big two manufacturers: Pampers, (800) 285-6064, and Huggies, (800) 544-1847.

~ *Kathie, South Carolina*

More Expensive Isn't Always Better

I use only cheap, disposable diapers (from Wal-Mart, Toys "R" Us, etc.), and they always work fine.

~ *Marilyn S., Parsippany, New Jersey*

Making Diapers Last Longer

I have a great solution to lengthen diaper duration: Diaper Doublers. If you've got a long stretch coming up when you just don't know if your diaper will last (for example, overnights) these are pads that you can stick in the diaper. Use one or two; if you've got a boy, fold them in half up front. It adds an amazing amount of liquid-holding capacity. And it can save you from dealing with those 4 A.M. crib changes.

~ *JohnmhIII*

Velcro: Friend or Foe?

I love the diapers with Velcro on them, but I am going to have to give them up. My four-month-old has figured out the whole Velcro thing. Apparently he would rather be naked!

~ *Marian H., Augusta, Georgia*

Tips for a Smoother Diaper Change

I have a three-month-old son, and for a while he kept having leaky diapers until I discovered that I needed to aim his penis straight toward the center. Now he rarely has a leaky diaper!

~ *Julie K., Powder Springs, Georgia*

To keep a wiggly infant from crawling off during diaper changes, hand her a nontoy plaything, such as a clean toothbrush or an empty cardboard container. This will keep her occupied until you get the diaper on.

~ *Noni B., Lafayette, Louisiana*

Here's what I do to make diaper changes more pleasant:

1. Put a radio by the changing table to play when it's time for a change. The music will soothe and distract the baby.

2. To keep baby wipes from drying out on the top, turn the container upside down every once in awhile. This will keep the wipes at the top moist and keep the bottom wipes from getting too soggy.

~ *Ann Marie M., Lincoln University, Pennsylvania*

DIARRHEA

Diarrhea isn't just a nuisance, it's an epidemic. Each year there are about one billion cases of diarrhea in children worldwide. Of course, in most cases (more than 990 million of them),

8. Recycle. If you're formula feeding, recycle the cans. Glass baby-food jars are reusable and can be recycled. You can keep any number of things in them, from leftovers to coins or paper clips.

9. Make your own baby wipes. [See page 76 for instructions.] Not only will you be reducing waste by avoiding the packaging that commercial wipes come in, but the paper towels are more biodegradable than wipes. And if you use recycled paper towels (they can be rougher, but you can use them to

wipe the baby's hands or your own), you're cutting down on trash even more.

10. Prevent litter. Take a trash bag along when you take your baby for a walk in the stroller. Not only will you get more exercise by bending to pick up trash, but you'll also beautify your regular walk. Bring along some homemade baby wipes to clean your hands before you handle your baby.

diarrhea will resolve by itself within a week or so. Still, diarrhea can cause dehydration (not to mention sore bottoms), so it's nothing to ignore. Here Dr. Greene explains what diarrhea is and how to treat it.

When Is It Diarrhea?

Q: My baby has been having four runny poops each day for the last five days (she normally goes once a day). Is this diarrhea? If it is, what should I do?

~ *Bob, California*

DR. GREENE'S INSIGHT

A: Here's how to tell it's diarrhea. Healthy baby poop is often soft and runny, and it occurs quite frequently (especially in the first month). One two-week-old with 10 runny stools a day may be perfectly healthy, yet a four-month-old with three stools a day, all firmer than the other baby's, may have diarrhea. So how can a parent tell?

Look for a sudden increase in the frequency of the stools. Each baby has her own stool frequency pattern that changes slowly over time. If it changes noticeably within only a few days, she may have diarrhea. Any baby who has more than one stool per feeding should also be suspected of having diarrhea, even if this isn't a sudden change. Also look for a sudden increase in the water content of the stool. Other signs of illness in your baby, such as poor feeding, a newly congested nose, or a new fever, make a diagnosis of diarrhea more likely.

Diarrhea in babies can be caused by a change in diet (including a change in the mother's diet if the baby is breastfed), by infection, by use of antibiotics, or by other illness.

Here's how to treat it. The central concern with diarrhea is the possibility of dehydration from loss of body fluids. Treatment is aimed at preventing dehydration, the real culprit. Most children with diarrhea can be safely treated at home.

If your breastfed baby develops diarrhea, don't stop nursing. Breastfeeding helps prevent diarrhea (making diarrhea only half as likely); it also speeds recovery (*Journal of Pediatrics*, May 1996).

If your baby is formula-fed, you might want to switch to a soy-based formula while the diarrhea lasts. A soy formula containing fiber (Isomil DF) can be even more effective at slowing down the stools (*Clinical Pediatrics*, March 1997). Do not dilute the formula.

For both breastfed and formula-fed babies who still seem thirsty when not feeding, supplement with an oral rehydration solution to prevent dehydration. (Pedialyte is the best-known solution, but other brands are also effective. Children in my practice seem to prefer the taste of chilled, grape-flavored KaoLectrolyte.)

If your baby is already old enough to be taking solid foods, then carrots, rice cereal, bananas, potatoes, and applesauce can help slow the stools. Avoid fruit juices, peas, pears, peaches, plums, prunes, and apricots until the stools are back to normal (usually within a week or so).

When to Contact Your Pediatrician

Contact your pediatrician right away if your baby

- won't drink or appears to be getting dehydrated (dry mouth, crying without tears, sunken soft spot, lethargic, or going eight hours without producing urine);

d diarrhea

TRIVIA QUESTION

This sugar, found in some fruit juices, has been shown to cause diarrhea in infants:

a. Sucrose

b. Fructose

c. Dextrose

d. Lactose

e. Sorbitol

Answer: e

- is under two months old and has diarrhea with a fever;

- vomits for 24 hours;

- has eight stools in eight hours; or

- has blood, mucus, or pus in the stool.

If the diarrhea lasts longer than a week or is accompanied by more than 72 hours of fever, be sure to get in touch with your pediatrician.

One final thought is to not forget your baby's bottom. Stool normally contains some of the enzymes that help us digest our food. When stool travels through the intestines more quickly, not only is there more poop but the poop also contains more of these enzymes, which can then start to "digest" the soft skin of your baby's bottom. Cut down on baby wipes during diarrhea. Frequent diaper changes, rinsing the bottom with water, air drying, and protective ointments and creams can be a real help.

Using Food to Treat Diarrhea

There is a diet that doctors prescribe for older babies and young children with diarrhea. It is known as the BRAT diet:

B = Bananas
R = Rice
A = Applesauce
T = Toast

These are binding foods and help firm up runny stools. They are all fairly bland foods, too, so it makes them a little more appealing to a tummy that isn't feeling well. It's recommended that anyone

From *Parent Soup: The Game.*
(Source: *American Baby,*
March 1, 1997)

experiencing diarrhea stick to this diet until passing at least two well-
formed stools.

~ *Lisa K., Tucker, Georgia*

 ## DOCTORS *(See also Fever, Head Bumps)*

Choosing your child's doctor is a big step. You trust this
person with your child's life. You want to believe that the
doctor knows what he or she is talking about, you must be comfortable
enough to tell him or her what you would like done—and you've got to
hope that once you find this miracle person you'll also learn that
treatment by this physician is covered under your insurance plan. No
problem, right? Well, it may not be easy, but if you're reading this right
now (which you are), you'll at least know how to decide.

DR. GREENE'S INSIGHT

One of the best ways to identify great doctors is to ask nurses in that field
whom they would recommend. Nurses see firsthand how physicians handle
medical crises and how they interact with people. If I were moving to a town
where I didn't know what pediatricians were great, I would call or drop by a
labor and delivery unit, a newborn nursery, or a pediatric ward at a local
hospital and ask several nurses for their opinions.

When considering a doctor, the big issues you want to think about are the
following four questions:

1. Is this a well-trained physician who stays current with medical trends?
   Determining a physician's qualifications is fairly simple and a good place

to start. If a doctor does not meet your standards, you can easily eliminate him as a candidate and move on. Here are some questions you can ask physicians to help you determine their qualifications:

● Where did they complete undergraduate school?

● Did they receive honors?

● What medical school did they attend?

● Where did they complete their residency?

● Did they serve as a Chief Resident? (If so, they were at the top of their class and judged to be good with people.)

● Are they board certified? (All physicians are licensed, but not all are certified.)

● What are they doing to continue training? (The AMA gives a "Physician's Recognition Award" to those in practice who actively pursue continuing education.)

While many excellent doctors didn't complete their educations at top-ranked schools, finding out their stories is still worthwhile. You may want to ask why they chose a particular medical school and a particular field of medicine. Probe about the methods they use to stay current with rapidly expanding medical knowledge. How they handle these questions will give you a lot of information.

2. Does this physician practice medicine in a way that agrees with your philosophy of health care? This is a much more subjective area than the first question. It requires you to determine the kind of physician you are looking for. Do you want a doctor who works with you to determine the best course for your health care, or are you more comfortable with a physician who simply tells you what to do? Do you prefer a minimalist approach to medicine, or do you want medical intervention whenever it may be appropriate? Are you excited about alternative medicine, or are you more comfortable with traditional Western medical practices? After you have answered these questions for yourself, you will be able to tailor the following questions to draw out the information you are seeking. Does the doctor

- provide patient education?

- give you treatment options?

- have a sensible approach to the use of antibiotics?

- consider alternative treatments, such as diet?

3. Does the physician's practice fit your practical needs? The practical aspects of a practice include office location, office hours, average waiting time for an appointment, and so on. They may not be important in determining what physician you select, but they are very important in determining if she or he will be able to serve the needs of your family:

- Is the office within a reasonable distance from your home?

d doctors

- What hours is the practice open? Any Saturdays or evenings?

- How long in advance must you schedule a physical? (This is tricky—if you have to schedule too far in advance, you are likely to become frustrated. On the other hand, if you discover there is no waiting, you might want to ask why—and whether the practice has just added an additional doctor, for instance.)

- Does the practice make same-day appointments for sick patients? Do they accept drop-ins for sick patients?

- If so, how long is the average wait?

- Does the doctor accept phone calls during office hours? (This often saves you a trip to the office.)

- How many doctors share after-hours on-call duties? If you have an after-hours need, will you be able to talk to one of the doctors from the practice? A doctor from another practice? A nurse? An answering machine?

- How does the practice handle after-hours, nonemergency needs? Is it associated with an after-hours clinic or do the physicians meet you in the emergency room? Or do they tell you to take two aspirins and call in the morning?

- How does the practice handle billing? Do the doctors require payment at the time of the visit, or do they bill your insurance company first and then bill you after receiving payment from your insurance? (This is not important if you have an HMO.)

4. Will you feel comfortable asking this doctor any health-related questions that might arise? Perhaps most important, notice the quality of your interaction with the physician. This can be more significant than the specific information imparted. You need to feel comfortable with this person, confident that she or he is genuinely interested in your child's problems, and encouraged that communication will flow smoothly in both directions. Be sure that the doctor listens to what you have to say.

After looking at this exhaustive list of questions, you may realize that no doctor will score 100 percent, so prioritize your concerns and select the best candidate. If you find the physician who is the best fit for your family only to look him or her up in your insurance company's handbook and discover that this doctor is not listed, don't give up! Call the doctor's office and ask to speak to the person who is in charge of insurance billing. Ask him or her if the doctor you want is now accepting patients with your insurance. If the doctor is not, ask if there is any creative solution to your problem. If they cannot help you in any way, ask for a list of insurers that they do accept. If you are paying directly for your insurance, you may want to consider changing

PARENT POLL

Are you concerned that your pediatrician overprescribes antibiotics for your child?

Of 941 total votes

yes — 51.86%

no — 48.14%

1 bowl = 100 parents

companies. If you are getting insurance through your employer, take the list to your employer and find out if they currently offer any of these options. If you are looking for a pediatrician for a new baby, in many cases you will have 30 days from the baby's date of birth to make changes in your benefits. During that time you might be able to change to an insurance company that works with the doctor you want to see. If you are not looking for a pediatrician for a newborn, you may have to wait until open enrollment at your place of employment to make a switch.

Now that patients have options, selecting a physician for our children or ourselves is not an easy undertaking. Still, the reward for our efforts can be a more meaningful physician-patient relationship than has ever before been possible.

Don't Settle

In my humble opinion it is crucial to have a pediatrician whom you are completely comfortable with. Even though change can be hard, keep trying until you get one you really like and relate to well.

~ *Kristine D., Menlo Park, California*

EAR INFECTIONS

In the United States more than 25 million visits to pediatricians each year relate to ear infections, and ear infections are the most common diagnosis in children. Luckily, Parent Soup's own Dr. Greene is an expert on this common ailment—he's written a book on the subject entitled, *The Parent's Complete Guide to Ear Infections*. Here he summarizes the causes of ear infections and their treatments:

DR. GREENE'S INSIGHT

There are two basic types of ear infection, and they behave very differently. Otitis media with effusion (OME) is the name given to fluid in the middle ear. Acute otitis media (AOM) is fluid in the middle ear plus pain, redness, and a bulging eardrum. Children with OME are often asymptomatic: OME is often discovered at well-child examinations. Children with AOM act sick, especially at night, often with a fever. After an episode of AOM, the child is often left with OME for several weeks.

Ear infections occur when bacteria enters the middle ear through the eustachian tube, a narrow channel that connects the inside of the ear to the back of the throat, just above the soft palate. The tube is designed to facilitate drainage so that secretions that are normally made in the middle ear don't build up and burst the thin eardrum. Tiny hair cells in the tube propel this mucous blanket like a conveyer belt to carry bacteria down the drain. The tube also functions to keep the air space in the middle ear at the same pressure as the air around us. In this way the eardrum can move freely, and our hearing is most effective.

When all is well, the tube is collapsed most of the time in order to protect the middle ear from the many organisms that live in the nose and mouth. Only when you swallow does a tiny muscle open it briefly to equalize the pressures and drain the ear secretions. If any bacteria make it into the ear, the drainage mechanism, helped by the little hair cells, should flush them out.

Ear infections are the result of the eustachian tube's not performing its job. When the tube is partially blocked, fluid accumulates in the middle ear.

e ear infections

Bacteria already there are trapped and begin to multiply. If the tiny hair cells are damaged (as by a cold virus), the mucous blanket can't help move the bacteria out.

What Are the Causes of Ear Infections?

Respiratory infections, irritants (especially cigarette smoke), and allergies all can inflame the lining of the eustachian tube, producing swelling and increased secretions. They can also cause enlargement of the glands near the opening of the tube, blocking flow at the outlet. Sudden increases in air pressure (during descents in an airplane or on a mountain road) can both squeeze the floppy tube closed and create a relative vacuum in the ear. Drinking while lying on one's back can block the slit-like tube opening. The increased mucus and saliva during teething can also get in the way. In addition, the last two decades of the 20th century have seen a dramatic rise in ear infections due largely to increased pollution and the prevalence of early childhood day care (where children are exposed to many respiratory infections).

Small children get more ear infections than older children or adults because the tube is still shorter, more horizontal, and straighter—a quick and easy trip for the bacteria. In addition, the tube is floppier, with a tinier opening, and therefore it is easier to block.

What Are the Best Treatments?

Although antibiotics are a wonderful, life-saving treatment, we have erred in their overuse. We know this because more and more strains of bacteria are becoming resistant to them and, hence, harder to treat. I believe that antibiotics are not always necessary in the treatment of ear infections.

That said, each type of ear infection, OME and AOM, has its own recommended treatment. In otherwise healthy children one to three years old with OME, the Department of Health and Human Services and the American Academy of Pediatrics recommend environmental measures (breastfeeding, avoiding cigarette smoke, and reconsidering day care) and either observation *or* antibiotics. If the fluid is still present 6 weeks later, they recommend further observation *or* antibiotics. Only if OME is still present after 12 weeks *and* there is a bilateral hearing loss of more than 20dB (decibels) do they recommend treatment with either antibiotics or surgical tube placement (although I would definitely try antibiotics before placing tubes). Millions of cases of OME are needlessly treated with too many rounds of antibiotics.

For children with AOM, new guidelines have been suggested by Jack Paradise, MD. Although his ideas are controversial, he has made an excellent attempt to define the new, wiser, middle ground of antibiotic use. He recommends considering five factors when deciding on therapy: the child's age (older children recover more easily than young children), the season (summertime infections clear most easily), the severity of the episode (mild infections rarely cause problems), the child's history of ear infections (the fewer episodes of AOM, the more likely each one will clear), and the initial response to antibiotics (prompt improvement is a good sign). If these five factors point to a mild case, he recommends limiting treatment to five days. If the infection continues to escalate and shows resistance to antibiotics, it might even be possible to withhold antibiotics and follow the infection with frequent ear examinations.

What About Tubes in the Ear?

The surgical procedure for placing tubes in the ears has become one of the most commonly performed operations of any kind. The procedure is a simple one. A tiny tube, with a collar on both ends (which looks like this:][) is slipped through a tiny incision in the eardrum. This pressure-equalization (PE) tube

placed in my second child when she was nine months old. She is two years old now and has been infection free!

~ Lori H.,

Duluth, Georgia

provides a temporary, extra eustachian tube to allow bacteria and fluid to drain from the middle ear. The procedure has been in widespread use since 1954 and is very safe—probably safer than driving to the hospital for the surgery.

There are four agreed-upon indications for PE tube placement:

1. Children with prolonged OME (or fluid in the ear) will benefit from tube placement; OME is the most common reason children get tubes. Tubes are often recommended after 12 weeks of OME, but occasionally as early as 6 weeks. In some situations, which I will discuss, waiting four to six months is appropriate.

2. Children with recurrent AOM (fluid in the ear accompanied by a red, bulging eardrum, pain, and often a fever) are candidates for tube surgery. These would be children who have had at least three episodes in six months, have then been placed on prophylactic antibiotics (low-dose antibiotics to prevent ear infections), and who still continue to have AOM. This is the second-most common reason tubes are placed.

3. Children with complicated AOM should get tubes. The complications are not common, but they include abscesses, facial nerve problems, or AOM that stays hot, red, painful, and bulging despite antibiotic therapy. The common situation after treatment for AOM, where the child still has fluid in the ears (OME), which gradually clears on its own, is not considered a complication.

4. Children with complicated OME should get tubes. These complications generally relate to prolonged retraction of the eardrum and its impact on the little bones of the middle ear. This is a rare reason for tube placement.

Early tube placement should be considered for children who have any type of preexisting hearing loss or balance disorder. Children who have any other communication or sensory difficulty (e.g., visual, developmental delay) are also candidates for early tubes. There is no reason to delay tubes for children with known craniofacial, structural problems predisposing them to recurrent infections (cleft palate, Down's syndrome, etc.). Ongoing pain calls for earlier placement of tubes. The season or time of year also affects the advisability of tubes. In the fall or early winter, a child's ears are likely to get worse over the ensuing months, rather than better, and early tube insertion may be warranted.

Some situations suggest further observation, rather than rushing to tubes. Children with OME in only one ear at a time (and who have normal language development and balance for their age) should be followed four to six months. The same is true for children with bilateral OME but only mild hearing loss (less than 20 decibels). Children for whom prophylactic antibiotics have resulted in a reduction in the frequency or severity of bouts of AOM also warrant further observation before tube placement. Children who are younger than one year old should delay tubes if other considerations permit. Many children will have a decrease in the frequency and severity of ear infections in their second year. Finally, ear infections clear more easily and recur less readily in the spring and summer, which suggests a possible delay.

ECZEMA

Eczema is a chronic skin condition in which sensitive skin is aggravated by certain triggers, such as allergies, dryness, or stress. Some frequent sources of dryness are too-frequent bathing and overexposure to central heat. Try to avoid both. You may have to experiment to learn what foods or environmental factors might be causing your baby's eczema. Read what has worked for a couple of other parents.

Homemade Remedy

My six-month-old son has eczema that comes and goes on his face. Recently I discovered a cure you can buy from the grocery store: fresh apples! Buy either the Fuji or Macintosh kind. Peel and chop an apple into small pieces. Microwave for two and a half minutes. Then puree it. Give it as solid food three times a day. As soon as I started feeding my son apples, his eczema cleared up within a matter of hours!

~ *Teresa, Oregon*

Alleviate the Dryness

My daughter developed eczema when she was three weeks old, and her doctor said no more than two baths a week and even then, not to use soap. Also, she recommended Eucerin lotion. I used it on her three times a day, and the eczema cleared up within a few days.

~ *Lee K., Felton, Delaware*

FAILURE TO THRIVE *(See Growth)*

FAMILY TIME

When you, your partner, and baby are going through feedings and changings and cooking and working and sleeping, you may start to wonder if you'll ever share a calm moment together. Well, if you wait for a quiet moment to spend some quality time as a family unit, you may be waiting a long time. Thankfully, some parents have found ways to come together, which they shared with us at Parent Soup. Try these ideas, and if you find your own way to create meaningful family time, by all means come online and let us know.

Story Time

Ever since our baby boy was born, my husband reads a chapter of a book aloud at his late night feeding (10 P.M. or so). We just finished Bunyan's *Pilgrim's Progress*. This helps my husband feel a part of the nursing experience and helps establish an evening routine for the baby, as well as introducing him to books and the English language. It's been a relaxing way for all of us to unwind at the end of our day.

~ *Lynn H., Indianapolis, Indiana*

Family Meal

Even though our daughter is only 10 months old, we are already trying to instill the family meal idea with her. She has her baby-food meal at the same time we eat, and we give her toys on her tray when she is finished, so she stays sitting with us until the meal is over. She gets to hear lots of conversation this way (good for her verbal development). Plus maybe she will see the family meal as she gets older as "the way things are supposed to be."

~ *Ann Marie M., Lincoln University, Pennsylvania*

Family Night

Sometimes the family dinner is hard to do if you or your spouse has to work late. So what we do is schedule a once-a-week "Family Night." Unless it is an emergency we *cannot* change it. And we all do something together as a unit.

~ *Kait S., Brooklyn, New York*

f family time

Letters to Baby

When I was pregnant, I researched traditions and baby lore to find a way to let my baby know how wanted it was. I came upon a long-time tradition of writing a letter to the child. And even if your baby's already been born, it's a great way to capture the excitement and fulfillment of being a new parent. It goes like this.

Family and friends write letters to the child, filled with advice, aspirations, feelings they have about the baby, and words of wisdom that may have influenced them at the crossroads in their lives. Some letters include investments, savings bonds, pictures, whatever the author wants. The letters are sealed and saved for when the child comes of age. When I wrote to my friends and family and asked them to participate, I couldn't believe the response. People were delighted and honored to share their input.

You can decide for yourselves when to have the child open the letters. We chose 16 years old, a time when guidance and family involvement can make a real impact.

~ *Christina O., Woodstock, Vermont*

Keeping a Family Album

When taking photos of your baby, remember to take turns holding camera and baby. Otherwise, you'll have hundreds of mom and baby photos, but not a single photo of dad and baby.

~ *Ann Marie M., Lincoln University, Pennsylvania*

FATHERS

No matter what your family situation is, every baby has a father. Sometimes it's hard for mothers to get out of the way and let dads handle the babies themselves. Conversely, sometimes dads just don't know what it's like to take care of a baby and may take a good mother for granted. How can you see to it that your baby benefits from the influence of both parents?

Set Aside Baby-Father Time

This may sound crazy, but I work part-time and I deliberately began to work one night a week so that my husband and son have some time to bond and so he will see what I do all day! It has made all the difference. It was really hard for me at first, but daddies can take care of baby—sometimes they have unusual problem-solving techniques, but they *can* do it all!

~ *Susie L., Kingsport, Tennessee*

Stay Out of the Way

I made it a point not to nag my husband to handle the baby "my way." From day one, I tried to let him do it his way. There are things he does that I would do differently, but he gets everything done. My daughter Kayla actually eats better for him sometimes! He has his own style, and they are comfortable together. And his style is much more relaxed, which can be a godsend when I am frantic and running around like a chicken with my head cut off.

~ *NiteKryme*

f fathers

DR. GREENE'S INSIGHT

To all dads who are looking to find their parenting styles, there are many ways to go about it. In any bookstore you can find several good resources for fathers, but the most important resource of all is locked up inside you. By spending some time alone, pen in hand, exploring what it means to be a great father to your children, you can unearth a goldmine.

I would begin by recalling your own father when you were a child, making a list of all the things you loved most about him. Remember what you respected and what you enjoyed. Conjure up times that you miss. Make a list of some of the best memories you had together. Take some time to treasure moments that touch you deeply when you think of him.

Next I would list the things about your dad that you wish had been different. Remember what irritated or bothered you, things he said or didn't say, things he did or didn't do. Take some time to jot down negative memories from childhood, experiences with your dad (or perhaps when your dad was absent) that are sad memories. What do you wish had or hadn't happened?

Having taken time to reminisce, you are primed to dream a little bit. From your perspective, what would a fantasy father be like? What ingredients are key to you? In as much detail as you can, write out what would make the ideal dad.

Here are three things I would then do with this list:

1. Share it with someone who is intimate with you, preferably your parenting partner. Most partners would be thrilled to talk with you about how to be an outstanding father.

2. Read through your list with another father. This may be difficult, but another's experience will be invaluable in your quest to be the best father you can be.

3. This may be the most difficult step. Share the list with yourself, not just this once, but every month. Once a month read through it again. See if fresh insights occur to you. Jot down what you have learned and new grist for memories that might come up as your child grows. One of the toughest things about being a father is that it's not a one-time insight but a steady process of being with your child.

When I talk with adults about their memories of their dads and with children about what they want from their dads, the wish that comes up most often is for dads to be around the family more. Kids want Dad to be with them, whether it's cleaning, playing, working, studying, or whatever. Second, I've found that kids wish their fathers would listen to them more. They often feel that Dad doesn't really understand. Active, supportive listening is an incredible gift to give your child. The third wish I hear is for dads to open up to their kids. Many people feel that they really don't know what is going on inside their father's head. Being open and sharing your feelings with your kids will give them an invaluable treasure. And it's never too early to start being a positive father figure. Make sure you spend time holding, talking with, feeding, changing diapers for, and playing with your babies. It will set the stage for a lifelong, healthy relationship.

FERTILITY AFTER GIVING BIRTH

One of the oft-quoted benefits of breastfeeding is that because the return of fertility is delayed in nursing mothers, it's a natural form of birth control. But depending on a variety of factors—primarily how much you are breastfeeding—it is still possible to ovulate (and thus get pregnant) while nursing. Here, three experts (a La Leche League counselor, a two-time mom, and Dr. Greene) explain how fertility works in nursing women.

When Will My Period Return?

Q: I have been happily nursing for eight months. Now I'm ready to get pregnant again, but I don't want to stop nursing. However, I've heard that as long as I'm nursing, I probably won't menstruate. At least, I haven't started to yet. How can I get my period back and keep nursing? Should I be worried because I don't have a period yet?

~ *Parent Soup member Zsazsagbr*

La Leche League Responds

A: The length of time between birth and the return of fertility varies from woman to woman; some women resume their menses at 3 months postpartum, whereas others do not resume menstrual cycles for 12 months or more. There are some things you can do to encourage the return of your cycles. Because the key to delaying the return of menstruation seems to be frequent nursing, day and night, you can try to have your baby go longer between feedings at night, with a six-hour stretch at night without nursing. Your baby will let you know if this works for her! Offering more solid foods and water may help with the spacing, but keep in mind that breast milk should still be her primary source of nourishment. In some cases, the reduced sucking at the breast due to solids is enough to cause fertility to return. Sometimes, however, even infrequent nursing is enough to prevent pregnancy. At that point, you would have to decide if weaning is an acceptable alternative for you and your family. Also, it is possible to ovulate before you get your first postpartum menstrual period, and thus it is possible to get pregnant without ever having had a period between babies.

No Period Doesn't Mean No Ovulation

When you return to fertility seems to be a combination of the frequency of nursing, exercise, nutrition, and plain old genetics. But above all, *don't* believe that breastfeeding and no period mean that you can't get pregnant. I was breastfeeding my daughter exclusively when I dropped an egg, which became fertilized before I ever knew what happened. My son is living proof!

~ *Cary O., Woodbridge, Virginia*

Pregnant While Breastfeeding?

Q: If you aren't having a period yet and are still nursing an infant, how or when can you accurately determine if you might be pregnant again?

~ *Parent Soup member Alane104*

DR. GREENE'S INSIGHT

A: Women certainly can become pregnant again before their periods resume, even if they are still nursing. More than 65 percent of nursing women are ovulating by the time their babies are six months old. If you become pregnant, you will usually first become aware of this by changes in the way you feel. You may notice yourself feeling decidedly more fatigued, perhaps having morning queasiness. A new phase of breast or nipple soreness may also signal another pregnancy.

A home pregnancy test is an excellent way to get an objective answer. It works by detecting (in your urine) a hormone (HCG) created by the new pregnancy. The test can give a positive result as soon as the day your period would have come (usually 14 days following ovulation). Because you have no idea when this might be, take a test if you feel that you might be pregnant. Hcg levels should be detectable within 17 days following inter-course that leads to conception. A negative test result does not necessarily rule out a pregnancy, but a positive one indicates you are almost definitely pregnant. If it is negative, try testing again in a couple of weeks. In the meantime, certainly take care of yourself as if you were pregnant.

FEVER

One of the leftover mind-sets of days gone by is that fever is an enemy to humans. Whether we first learned of this through a novel (remember reading *Little Women* with horror as Beth slipped away?) or through family lore (your Great-aunt Helen was never the same after she had scarlet fever as a child), the fear of early childhood fevers remains. In this section, Dr. Greene helps dispel some of the dread and explains the function of fever as a defense mechanism and treatment for a baby who's battling illness.

DR. GREENE'S INSIGHT

I was surprised to learn in medical school that fever, far from being an enemy, is an important part of the body's defense against infection. While a fever signals to us that a battle might be going on in a child's body, the fever is fighting *for* the child, not against.

Most bacteria and viruses that cause infections in humans thrive best at 98.6 degrees Fahrenheit (37 degrees Celsius). Raising the temperature a few degrees can give the body the winning edge. In addition, a fever activates the body's immune system, accelerating the production of white blood cells, antibodies, and many other infection-fighting agents.

Parents' Fears About Fevers

Many parents fear that fevers will cause brain damage. Brain damage from a fever will not occur unless the temperature is above 107.6 degrees Fahrenheit (42 degrees Celsius) for an extended period of time. Many also fear that untreated fevers will keep going higher and higher, up to 107 degrees Fahrenheit or even more. Untreated fevers caused by infection will seldom go over 105 degrees unless the child is overdressed or trapped in a hot place. The brain's thermostat will stop the fever from climbing above 106 degrees Fahrenheit. Some parents fear that fevers will cause seizures. For the great majority of children this is not the case. About 4 percent of children, though, will sometimes have seizures with fever. These febrile seizures are caused by a rapid increase in temperature, not by the height of the temperature. In any event, febrile seizures are over in moments, with no lasting consequences. Treating fevers early in these children may prevent further febrile seizures.

What Temperature Constitutes a Fever?

While 98.6 degrees is considered the normal core body temperature, this value varies among individuals and throughout the day. The daily variation is minimal in children under six months of age, is about one degree in children six months to two years old, and gradually increases to two degrees per day by age six. A person's baseline temperature is usually highest in the evening. Body temperature, especially in children, is normally raised by physical activity, strong emotion, eating, heavy clothing, elevated room temperature, and elevated humidity. A rectal temperature up to 100.4 degrees Fahrenheit (38 degrees Celsius) may be entirely normal (no fever). A rectal temperature of 100.5 or

f fever

TRIVIA QUESTION

All of the following are
smart ways to treat your
child's fever, except

a. Keeping your child
   cool

b. Increasing fluid intake

c. Giving over-the-
   counter fever
   reducers

d. Sponging with tepid
   water

e. Withholding food

Answer: e

*Because fever raises the
caloric requirement, sick
babies need more than the
usual serving.*

From *Parent Soup: The Game*

above should be considered a fever. Lower values might indicate a fever,
depending on the child.

How to Treat a Fever

A fever does not necessarily need to be treated. If a child is playful and
comfortable, drinking plenty of fluids, and able to sleep, fever treatment is not
likely to be helpful. Steps should be taken to lower a fever if the child is
uncomfortable, vomiting, dehydrated, or having difficulty sleeping. The goal is
to bring the temperature between about 100 and 102 degrees—not to eliminate
the fever.

When trying to reduce a fever, first remove excess clothing or blankets.
The environment should be comfortably cool (one layer of lightweight clothing
and one lightweight blanket to sleep). Two medicines are useful for reducing
fever in children: acetaminophen (Tylenol) and ibuprofen (Children's Advil or
Motrin). Acetaminophen is given every four to six hours and works by turning
down the brain's thermostat. Don't use acetaminophen for a child under three
months of age without first having the child examined by a physician. Ibuprofen
is given every six to eight hours and helps fight the inflammation at the source
of the fever. It is not approved for children under six months. Both medicines
may be given for stubborn fevers, but be very careful about using the correct
dose of each.

A lukewarm bath or sponge bath may also help cool a febrile child (give the
bath after medication—otherwise the temperature bounces right back up). Avoid
cold baths or alcohol rubs: they cool the skin but often cause shivering, raising
the core body temperature and making the situation worse.

When to Call the Doctor

Any child under 90 days old with a fever should be examined by a physician
right away (unless a DPT shot was given in the previous 24 hours). Children of

any age who have a fever greater than 105 degrees should also be seen, unless the fever comes down readily with treatment and the child is comfortable. Any child who has a fever and is very irritable or confused, has difficulty breathing, has a stiff neck, won't move an arm or leg, or has a seizure should also be seen right away.

Even without such symptoms, children under six months of age with a fever should be examined by a physician within 24 hours (unless they just had a DPT), because they may have some infection that needs to be treated. Older children with a fever (6 to 24 months old) who are acting well and have no other symptoms should be seen if the fever lasts more than 48 hours.

While caring for your child with a fever, remember that fever is a friend: it alerts us to potential problems, activates the immune system, and fights bacteria and viruses.

GAS *(See also Crying and Colic)*

It's not just a natural resource. Gas is a serious source of discomfort in babies. And as this discomfort can cause babies to cry, it is also a serious concern for parents. (For tips on easing the crying, see pages 68–70.) To alleviate a possible source of the problem, try these remedies that worked for other lucky parents.

Natural Gas Relievers
Gassy?? Lay him on his back and gently bend his knees and push them *gently* up toward his belly. This should help relieve some gas. Also hold him in your arms on his back and just gently rub his belly in a circular motion. This, in addition to Mycilon drops, always relieves my baby.

~ *Jennifer T., Linthicum, Maryland*

My son did nothing but scream and cry for the first six months of his life. He was so gassy, it was just terrible. The doctor just kept saying it was colic until an associate saw him and diagnosed him with reflux. He was put on all sorts of medication and then was throwing up, still miserable and still gassy. Finally, I decided to do for him what I do for myself—I went to the health-food store and replaced all medications with herbs. There's a natural gas remedy for kids, Bubble Be Gone, that works wonders. I couldn't believe the turnaround in only a few days. He went from miserable baby to happy baby.

~ *Jane, Florida*

GETTING AROUND *(See also Travel)*

How old does the baby have to be before you can take her out? When can you start interacting with the world at large? Well, if the baby was born in the hospital and is now at home, she's already made her first excursion. If what you need is time outside the homestead, whether to pick up some milk at the store or to regain your sanity, Parent Soup moms can help you go out and get it.

When You're About to Climb the Walls

Q: I am a stay-at-home mom, breastfeeding my two-and-a-half-month-old baby. I would like to start going places (like to a movie with friends), but I worry about what would happen if I get delayed and my baby gets hungry while I'm gone.

~ *Debra D., Portland, Oregon*

La Leche League Responds

A: It is a big adjustment to add a new baby to the family. Your baby is lucky that you are able to be home with him and are breastfeeding him. Mothers often feel trapped by a new baby and feel as if they need to get away by themselves. But many mothers have found that until a baby becomes mobile at about six months, they are the perfect companion for a movie with husband or friends. Try carrying him in a sling and taking him to the movies with you, and you may find that just being with your friends and out of the house is all you really needed. In the dark theater you can nurse without anyone being the wiser. If anyone gives you annoyed looks, just smile and say, "If he cries, I promise we'll leave."

If you really do need to leave him for a little while, express small amounts of milk at a time until you've built up to a full feeding. You can express some milk, freeze it, and at another time express some more. Chill it and then add it to the bottle of frozen milk: don't add body- or room-temperature milk to frozen milk. After the first time you are gone, you will have extra milk and can then express that. Good luck.

When to Head Out

I took my two-month-old out when he was less than a week old. I take him out all the time now, to the grocery, to the mall, and for walks around the neighborhood. I need to get out, and he loves it, too. My only rule is that I don't take him out if it's below freezing. So go out and have fun with your kids!

~ *Sharon S., Jonesboro, Georgia*

THE BEST BAGS AND CARRIERS

I could not do without my Over-the-Shoulder Baby Holder. I bought it at a local street fair. La Leche League also sells them. I still use mine for my 15-month-old, 25-pound little boy. It was indispensable when he was little. And it was great for nursing: I was able to feed my baby while I was shopping at the mall, and no one could tell what we were up to!

~ *Debbie, Arizona*

I loved my Snugli baby carrier. I didn't like the sling, and my husband wouldn't be caught dead using it. I highly recommend a backpack

How to Carry Your Child

I have carried my son in a sling since he was born. Not only has it helped with colic—he's seven months now and still loves it. I wear him when we go for walks or to the mall. He loves being right there with me and seeing a different view of the world.

~ *Staci B., Rockville, Maryland*

I have a baby sling and would recommend it to anyone who will listen to me. My daughter didn't like the front pack, and it hurt my back because it felt like carrying a sack of potatoes. The sling gives you position options and disperses the weight. And it is a lifesaver for my four-and-a-half-month-old. I know what I will buy my friends for baby showers.

~ *Kait S., Brooklyn, New York*

Keeping Baby Germfree

When I was out with my baby and people stopped to admire him, I would politely ask them to "look, not touch." I felt a little funny about doing this, but hands spread germs, and I didn't want him to get sick. I found most people were very understanding.

~ *Susan H., Syracuse, New York*

What to Take with You

I buy washcloths in bulk, and every time I leave the house, I put four or five in a baggie with a little baby soap and water for any inevitable accidents that might happen. I also carry an empty baggie to put dirty washcloths in.

~ *Jeanine L., Folsom, California*

Possible Roadblocks and How to Avoid Them

When my first daughter was seven weeks old, I accidentally locked her inside the car. We live in Arizona, and in June it was already in the 100s. I ran into a restaurant and called 911 while my brother and mother (thank God they were there) went to work on the window. My brother finally broke it right before the fire truck got there. I was hysterical!!! The firemen were great; they said they would've broken the window, too, and that I was not a bad mom—that this happens all the time. Since then, I have made a car key and a house key and pinned them in my diaper bag. Since I grab my purse and bag before the baby, I haven't had a lock problem since. And the baby slept through the whole thing!

~ *Linda S., Mesa, Arizona*

GETTING BACK INTO SHAPE

So you have come home from the hospital with a beautiful new baby—and, more than likely, a not-so-beautiful (in your eyes) new body. Try to remember that it took your body nine months to gain the weight (not to mention give life to a magnificent new creature), so cut yourself some slack and admit that it will take at least that long for the weight to come off. Even more important to keep in mind is the fact that since your body is capable of giving life, it deserves your utmost respect and gratitude, no matter how much your stomach now sags.

That being said, there are smart and sane ways to start an exercise program that will help you blow off steam, tone up your body, and fit back into your old clothes. Here are some tips from our members:

also. Diaper bags that go on your shoulder just don't work when you also have baby in your arms. And, my husband is much more willing to carry a backpack than a diaper bag.

~ *JLJMARKIS*

We love Land's End diaper bags. Ours has lasted through two babies! The fact that they do not have ducks or teddies on them is great for dads.

~ *SDupuis128*

Cut Yourself Some Slack

When I was pregnant, everyone told me that I would probably leave the hospital in my old jeans because of all the exercising I did during the pregnancy. I was totally shocked after I had given birth to a seven-pound baby girl and got on the scale: I had lost only five pounds. Today (three months later) I am still ten pounds over my prepregnancy weight, I have a jelly belly, and every time I step down my thighs provide lovely slapping sound effects. I had been so obsessed with getting back into my clothes that I was losing sight of what was really important—my daughter and her happiness. I do work out every now and then, and it's important to exercise because it releases the stresses of motherhood. However, I am finally realizing that it is not what clothes I fit into but whether my daughter is emotionally provided for! I would love to have a flat stomach, thin thighs, and a butt that doesn't hit my ankles, but I wouldn't trade that for my daughter's health and well-being.

~ *Nancy O., Bernardsville, New Jersey*

Bring Your Baby Along

I did not start losing those 50 pounds I had gained during my pregnancy until I realized that I had to involve my baby daughter in my workout or not work out at all. The term *workout* is not really accurate. All we did was walk briskly (well, she rode in her stroller) for two miles on a trail around a local park each day. It was a different adventure every day. I started doing this when Yasmeen was five months old.

At first, she sat quietly in the stroller and often fell asleep during the walk. Later, she needed to bring along several toys, which she would throw out of the stroller when she was done with them. This involved a different kind of exercise for me: stop, bend over, pick up toy, place it in stroller basket, resume walking for two minutes; stop, pick up toy. . . . Admittedly, this is not an ideal workout, but at least I am able to stick with it better than my earlier plans to go for a run every other evening when my husband could watch Yasmeen.

Involving your baby in your exercise plans actually makes it more likely that you will stick to your routine. You are less dependent on your partner or another person responsible for watching your baby. Eventually, you also start enjoying the opportunity to be outside every day with your baby. I used to love pointing out every little thing (tree, squirrel, bird, trash, old beer bottle) to Yasmeen. The true reward comes on the day when they start pointing and babbling back to you. It can be mommy-baby special time like no other. Oh, yes, and you also lose some of those pounds in the process, but who cares about that when you are having fun?

~ *Noni B., Lafayette, Louisiana*

Exercises You Can Do Anywhere

I have found that isolation exercise works wonders. Pull in your abdominal muscles and tighten. Hold for a count of 10. Release and do again. You can do this anywhere, but don't forget to breathe!

~ *Mimi L., Frederick, Maryland*

Why a Gym Is Worth the Money

I joined the local gym and go to abs classes pretty faithfully, and it helps a lot. The best part is that they baby-sit the kids for free. It's a wonderful break in the day.

~ *Parent Soup member BuddhaFrog*

Motivation Loves Company

A group of us in our office all had our babies within two or three months of each other. We get together at lunch and power-walk for about half an hour. We also talk about what's going on with our kids. It's great motivation to get out there and do something.

~ *Stacy, California*

Prior to starting a jogging program with my coworkers on my lunch hour, I could not find the time to exercise: I was always tired and felt discouraged. Now I am very optimistic because I have regained my energy, and my endurance is up—a major bonus of regular exercise.

~ *Karen, Maryland*

There are some precautions to heed until your body gets back to its previous strength:

Easy on the Abs

Most postpartum women have diastasis, a vertical separation of the abdominal rectus muscle. You can check yourself to see if you have it. Lie on the floor with your knees bent to support your back. Place your hand flat over your belly button, fingers pointed down toward your feet, and start an abdominal crunch (modified sit-up) as high as you can. If you see or feel your fingers separate more than two fingers' width (a little is normal), you've got the separation. It takes six weeks to six months for the muscle to heal, and it must be exercised *gently* during that time! Overdoing it could cause lifelong problems. Modify your crunches by holding the muscles with your hands (cross your hands and place them on either side of your stomach muscles and pull them to the center) or by taking a sheet to use as a belt around your entire waist or abdominal area and pulling the crossed-over ends outward and upward as your exercise.

~ Nancy, Texas

Give Yourself Time to Heal

Start slow and listen to your body. Remember that your joints, especially your hips, are still loose, and it is easier to injure yourself now than prepregnancy. Work out like you did when you were pregnant, and only increase the strenuousness of your workouts as your body permits.

~ Amy A., Costa Mesa, California

Despite your best efforts, however, your body may never be the same as it was prepregnancy. Sure, we all know of someone who still looks like a model despite three kids. You know how that inner voice works ("But Stephanie Seymour returned to modeling for Victoria's Secret within months of her second child"). There's only one word for that rationale: ugh. At some point you simply have to thank whoever or whatever you thank (God, Allah, Buddha, Isis, Ra, the ancient sun god) for your children—and start buying pants with an elastic waist.

Hello, Belly

I have two children, both by C-section. I exercise regularly, and my belly never leaves. I think that having a C-section is like opening a factory-packed box. You can never put all the parts back in right.

~ Leigh, New York

Who Said This Was Easy?

Everyone told me I would lose the weight right away while I was breastfeeding. "The pounds will melt off while breastfeeding." Ha! I just

---

TRIVIA QUESTION

How much weight can a woman expect to lose when her child is born?

a. 5–7 pounds

b. 8–10 pounds

c. 12–14 pounds

d. 16–20 pounds

e. 25–30 pounds

Answer: c

There is no justice. Although we've all heard about the woman who swore she lost 50 pounds in the delivery room, very few of us have ever met her.

From Parent Soup: The Game

SUGAR-FREE RECIPE

I lost a lot of weight just by cutting sugar out of my diet, and I have a terrible sweet tooth! But here's one of my favorite recipes:

OATMEAL RAISIN COOKIES

1 cup whole-wheat flour
¾ cup wheat germ
½ cup rolled oats
1 tablespoon baking powder
2 teaspoons cinnamon
1 cup apple juice concentrate
¼ cup vegetable oil
1 egg
¾ cup raisins

Preheat oven to 375 degrees Fahrenheit. Coat two cookie sheets with vegetable cooking spray. Set aside. Mix the flour, wheat germ, oats, baking powder, and

wanted everyone to know that you're not the only one who didn't lose a ton while nursing.
~ *Kristi M., Dallas, Texas*

Importance of Hugability

What would you rather hug, a barbie doll or a teddy bear? If I were a baby, I would definitely opt for the teddy bear!
~ *Angela G., Alabaster, Alabama*

Favorite Exercise Videos

Many moms on the Parent Soup message boards have found that they are more likely to exercise if they don't have to leave the house to do it. Here they share their favorite exercise videos, so that you, too, can start working on your form.

- *FIRM videos*—they're pretty challenging, so if you've never worked out, take it slow with them.
  ~ *Kala C., Dallas, Texas*

- *Reebok Winning Body Workout*—this video went right to work on my postbaby bowl full of jelly body. And you don't have to look at women with perfect shapes; everyone in this is very real.
  ~ *Candice C., New York, New York*

- *Super Abs of Steel*—this video will kick you into high gear. Don't be surprised if you can't do the whole tape at first.
  ~ *Parent Soup member ManeKelly*

- *Jane Fonda's Complete Workout*—it's got fun songs and dances that make you feel great, as well as a good ab-crunching segment and stretching in the second half.

  ~ Parent Soup member MargLebrun

- *Step Reebok*—a good workout, and fun, too!

  ~ Sarah M., Cedar Falls, Iowa

- Karen Voight, *Energy Sprint*—one of the most challenging and best workouts I've had!

  ~ Sarah M., Cedar Falls, Iowa

- *Buns of Steel* tapes (the 15-minute workouts)—perfect if you don't have a lot of time. Each workout lasts only 15 minutes!

  ~ Carole, Tennessee

Lactic Acid in Breast Milk

Q: I have recently begun to exercise again (I have a seven-week-old baby) and am worried about lactic acid buildup's possibly interfering with nursing. I've heard that the buildup may cause breast milk to be less appealing to the baby or cause the baby to get gas. Has anyone else heard this? And if so, what do you do about it?

  ~ Mary Jane R., Somerville, New Jersey

A: I've heard that you should nurse the baby right before you exercise. By the time you nurse again, the lactic acid buildup has gone down.

  ~ Kristi M., Dallas, Texas

cinnamon in a large mixing bowl. Combine the juice concentrate, oil, egg, and raisins in a blender. Blend at medium speed until the raisins are chopped. Pour the mixture into the dry ingredients and stir together. Drop the batter by heaping teaspoons onto the prepared sheets, about one inch apart. Flatten each mound with the back of a fork. Bake, being careful not to let the cookies become too brown and crispy, about 8 to 10 minutes. Let the cookies cool slightly on the sheets before removing them to a plastic bag. This will prevent the cookies from becoming hard. Wait until cookies are completely cool before sealing the plastic bag. Continue until all cookies are baked. Cookies can be frozen.

  ~ Lori G., South River, New Jersey

GOING BACK TO WORK
(See also Child Care)

You may need the money, you may need the interaction with adults, or you may need the satisfaction that comes from getting paid for your talents. For whatever reason, you're going back to work. What follows is some practical advice—from how to dress when none of your clothes fit, to how to keep breastfeeding, to how to make the most of your time with your baby. (As for who will take care of your baby while you're gone, see Child Care.)

Help! My Clothes Don't Fit!

Q: I gained 40 pounds during my pregnancy. My newborn is now four weeks old and I've lost only 25 pounds. Despite my best efforts, I cannot get into any of my clothes, or shoes for that matter (how weird!). I'm going back to work in two months, and I'm eager to go shopping for new clothes. Should I buy my old size and pray that I'll return to it, or should I do something in between?

~ Ziette, New York

A: I heard of a woman who just went back to work and couldn't fit into all her work clothes yet, so she picked a few things to get her through the transition. Why waste the money? I know for me, I feel very bad about myself if my clothes are too tight—the feeling lasts all day, and no one needs that when she's trying to lose weight. Get some things that fit and make you feel good about yourself (and are machine washable, if you have a "spit-upper" as I do!), and just keep working toward your old size. Some of

your clothes may never fit the way they did. But the payoff is
definitely worth it!

   ~ *Kait S., Brooklyn, New York*

A: My advice on clothing (based on gaining 60 pounds during pregnancy
and not losing all of it until 18 months later) is knits! In patterns—
and with elastic or loose fit. Don't buy your old size; wearing tight
clothes is uncomfortable and depressing. I have found that with
elastic waists and jackets or cardigans, I can wear anything from my
usual size 8 to a size 12. Also, I got a few dresses from the Motherwear
catalog (for breastfeeding access), and they were wonderful—
adjustable fit, not too tight, but not maternity clothes. Keep in mind
that your shape may never be the same again. My breasts are still
larger and my tummy rounder, even though my weight is the same as
it was prepregnancy. The doctor told me that pregnancy hormones
allow your tendons to loosen, which explains your larger shoe size.
They might not shrink back. So definitely buy some shoes that fit—
you need comfortable shoes for lugging babies!

   ~ *Kait S., Brooklyn, New York*

How to Keep Breastfeeding While Working Outside the Home

I nursed both my boys after I went back to work part-time. Here are a
few words of wisdom. First, get a good breast pump. After my second son
was born, my employer provided a hospital-grade pump for use at work.
It was wonderful. It pumps both sides at once and is painless and
efficient. If this is an option, go for it! I also had good luck with a
battery-operated pump called Gentle Expressions. It cost only about $40.

   In regard to when to pump, when I was trying to stockpile milk, I
often pumped one side while I nursed on the other. This works well

because you get the letdown more easily. It can be an acrobatic feat, however!

One last bit of advice. If you plan on introducing a bottle, don't wait until the week before you go back to work. I made that mistake with my first son. I started sooner with my second son (about four weeks), and it went much more smoothly.

~ Angela H., Oceanside, California

I work full-time and pumped for my daughter for six months. It was getting to become a hassle, and I seemed to be pumping less and less milk. I quit pumping at work and gave her formula only when she was at the sitter's. We nursed on the weekends and in the morning and night on weekdays. I had no problems feeding her on the weekends, and she seemed content with the amount of milk I was producing. Mondays I was a little fuller than usual, but not uncomfortable or leaky. We did this until she was almost 12 months, when she decided she did not want to nurse anymore. I missed it more than she did!

~ Nanci W., Port Orange, Florida

Q: I am a first-time, new mom. My precious baby is three weeks old, and I have to go back to work when she is six weeks old. I have been trying to nurse, but it is not going well at all! She eats a little bit and then goes to sleep. As soon as I put her down, she wakes up and wants to nurse again. I can't get anything done, and I don't get to sleep very much. I'm really afraid that I won't be able to keep this up when I go back to work. Will it hurt her health too much if I change her over to a bottle?

~ Dorothy T., Trenton, New Jersey

DR. GREENE'S INSIGHT

A: I can see how you would feel like giving up, but there are so many benefits from nursing that I encourage you to try the following suggestions before deciding. Your daughter has fallen into a common pattern of "nibble nursing." Because of this, she never gets really full—she wakes up when you put her down because she is still hungry. The way to solve this problem requires help, ideally from your daughter's father. If that is not possible, you will need the help of a loving, supportive family member or friend. Your support person may need to spend an entire day and night with you. The sooner you can arrange to do this, the better.

If your daughter is nibbling frequently, you may currently not be producing enough milk to satisfy her. In order to increase your milk supply, you will need to begin pumping your breast milk after each daytime feeding. (You need to get as much rest as possible, so I do not recommend pumping at night.) When you pump, you are sending a signal to your body that it needs to make more milk to keep up with your baby's needs. Miraculously, your body will start to produce more milk to meet the demand.

It is important that you do not feed your baby more often than every hour and a half to two hours on an ongoing basis. By forcing her to wait when she is hungry, she will be determined to eat more when she has the chance. As a result, she will get full and be able to sleep for a longer period. Sometimes the turnaround takes as little as one cycle!

If you do not yet make enough milk to satisfy her needs, you can use the milk you have pumped to supplement breastfeeding. Preferably, have someone else give her a bottle immediately after nursing, to "top her off."

If your daughter is used to eating on demand, she will not like being forced to wait. If she becomes fussy before the appropriate time for nursing, you may need to physically leave the house so that you can maintain your

121

commitment to not nursing her until the hour and a half is up. This is another reason why you need a support person—to have someone present with her while you are gone.

I understand how overwhelming the situation feels right now. Sleep deprivation is a large part of that, so while your support person is there to help you, get as much rest as you can. Even after your support person leaves, take a nap every time your daughter does. You may feel that napping is being lazy, but it's not. By doing so you will have a more positive outlook on your situation, and you will be able to produce more milk to meet your daughter's needs.

Making the Most of Your Time Together

Q: I have a seven-week-old and I'm returning to work Tuesday (pout). My daughter practically lives in her swing, and I'm wondering what other things I can do to keep her occupied. I am starting to feel terrible at the thought of working all day, then spending most of our time together with her in the swing. I will usually put a blanket on the floor and bring her down there with me, but what else can I try?
~ *Tiffany W., Monroe, Michigan*

A: Nursery rhymes are great for this age. "This Little Piggie" helps her find her toes. Touch her hands to different textures, use words to describe them. Talk to your baby, mirror her sounds as she begins to babble. Play peekaboo, even though it's more peek than boo at this age. Stick out your tongue; she will mimic you. This is so much fun with a new baby. Even a baby only hours old will do it back. Take a toy and move it close to her and then a couple of feet away. As it gets closer, she will start to reach for it as she gets more coordination.

Dance with her. It's a fantastic thing to do with a baby—exposure to music and movement will help her later on with walking and talking.
~ *Tarrant F., Eugene, Oregon*

GRANDPARENTS

While you are going through your transition to parent, your parents are going through the transition to grandparent. Even if this isn't their first grandbaby, they are still remapping their emotions to include love for your new child. Like all transitions, this one might not necessarily be smooth. A frequent complaint about grandparents on Parent Soup's message boards is that they are quick with a comment such as, "I burped/fed/changed/(fill in the blank here) you differently, and you turned out OK." And they are slow to praise you in your new role. To top it off, all those hormones coursing through your veins make you extra sensitive. Take a *deeeeeeep* breath. There are actually some people out there who've found a way to smooth out strained family relations after the birth of the new baby, and they're here now to tell us how they did it. Try to remember how important your grandparents were to you (or how you wish they were more so). Then sit back and let that relationship happen, even if sometimes you have to bite your tongue.

When Your Parents Intrude

Q: My mother is obsessed with my baby. It started when I got pregnant, but it's become worse. She hogs the baby. She stops by to visit us every weekend. She comes by even when we ask her not to (when we want to have some time alone with the baby). She calls him her baby, and of course she's always telling me how she would do things differently. I love my mother, but she is making me crazy. Am I the only person with this problem?

~ *Linda O., New York, New York*

Possible Solutions

A: You could suggest to your mother that she volunteer some time at a local hospital in the pediatrics or neonatal wards. There are lots of babies and children who would love a "grandmother" to come and read them stories and play games with them. In the neonatal ward there are babies who need to be held in order to continue to thrive. I did this for a while, and it means so much to the children. Your mother could bond with them and they could have great friendships.

~ *Carol N., Rialto, California*

A: My husband's mom was the same way! When I was pregnant, she bought everything, including the crib. She arranged the baby's room and picked the theme. Some people thought that I was crazy for getting mad, but it was an invasion on me! She then started to refer to the baby as hers! I finally told her that I appreciated everything she had done, but enough is enough; just because she did all those wonderful things, she was not entitled to the baby! I had to be stern, but she's changed considerably since then, and we are getting along much better.

~ *Linda, Pennsylvania*

A: I had and still have minor skirmishes with my mother-in-law, but I have learned to be a little stronger. I realized that her comments hurt me so badly because I really cared what she thought of me, and I really wanted to be seen as a good mother. Now, when she makes a comment, like "You need to get him on a bottle," I flat out tell her that I'm not planning on doing that. I'm not mean about it, and I don't treat it like a power struggle. Now, instead of commenting on my parenting skills, she does things like buy my son tons of clothing and toys. I just take them with a smile and realize that this is her way of making sure she's important in my son's life. She doesn't understand that she doesn't need to buy him things for him to love her. I still resent her sometimes, but I've helped alleviate some of the tension between us by making it a point to ask her advice about small things (e.g., "Do you think I should try carrots or peas first?"). I also say things like, "He loves you so much," or "He pointed at your picture yesterday." She really eats that up. Mostly, I've just realized that no matter what anyone says, I'm an excellent mother and I have a very happy little baby. I think that's the most important thing that mothers need to recognize about themselves.

~ *Lisa K., Dearborn, Michigan*

Other Side of the Coin

A new baby brings enough change in our lives, without having to also worry about a mother's response. Sometimes I think our mothers feel guilty about the way they raised their own kids, so they go overboard to prove that they can be exceptional grandmas.

~ *Sam S., Summit, New Jersey*

After having my baby, I tried for about a month to breastfeed. My mother-in-law was holding my hand through labor, and she came home with us and helped me and told me I should give my baby a bottle. Due to all the hormones, this really upset me and I took it personally. Sometimes mothers-in-law try to help, but it only makes you feel worse. My mother-in-law was with me just 10 weeks ago when my baby was born, and last week she died of cancer. What a brave lady to fly halfway across the country to hold my hand when she was so sick herself. None of us had any idea how sick she was. Now I feel awful for thinking that she didn't care about my feelings. All I know is that she loved me and she loved the baby, and her grandson is really going to miss out on a great grandmother. I really miss her. So sometimes people who care about you might hurt your feelings, for whatever reason, but they do love you and it's not worth getting upset over! I only hope I can be such a good mother-in-law when my son grows up and gets married.

~ *Loraine T., Dallas, Georgia*

Magical Power of Grandparents

I just got back from a vacation and found out something pretty funny: while we were gone our son ate all sorts of stuff he doesn't usually eat. Now, some of that was your typical grandma feeding cookies, juice, and so on. Sigh. But he also ate lots of steamed broccoli, cauliflower, asparagus, you name it. She said she made little broccoli trees and then put them on a separate plate out of his reach on the table. He just looked at it for a while and then asked for the "trees." Of course, I tried this when we got home and it didn't work.

~ *Amy A., Costa Mesa, California*

We were going to visit my mother when my daughter was 10 months. Mom asked if she should stock up on anything. I told her she just eats what we eat, but be sure to have some applesauce and fruit. My mother said she would get some bananas, and I told her anything but that: my daughter hated bananas. Well, Mom had bananas in her house and my daughter practically begged for them. One afternoon she ate six in a row!

126

Grandmothers must sprinkle some special dust over food to make it attractive to children.

~ *Tarrant F., Eugene, Oregon*

GROWTH

New parents can talk for hours about how much their babies weigh and at what percentile that weight falls on a growth chart. If you are concerned about your baby's weight, you are no exception to the rule. (Come check out our message boards for proof!) Remember that it is normal for a baby to lose 5 to 10 percent of his body weight in the week or so after birth. The only cause for concern is when he doesn't gain it back in a timely manner. Dr. Greene explains:

What Causes "Failure to Thrive"?

Q: What are some possible causes of the very general diagnosis of "failure to thrive"? At seven weeks, our daughter is still seven and a half ounces below her birth weight, and none of the "experiments" our doctor has suggested has helped her gain any weight. We were advised to try eliminating all dairy products from my diet, then to supplement with formula after each breastfeed, and later to give up nursing entirely and use formula feeding, but none of these is making a difference.

~ *Angela, Ohio*

DR. GREENE'S INSIGHT

A: When I see a new baby in my office for her first visit, the parents often get more excited about finding out their child's weight than just about anything else. The scale becomes the focus of the visit.

g growth

~~~~~~

This deep-rooted concern makes sense: In the first four to six months, a baby typically doubles her birth weight. She will triple her birth weight by the time she is a year old. Maximal brain growth also occurs during the first six months of life—the brain grows as much during a child's first year as it will during the entire rest of her life.

A child is "failing to thrive" when she is not growing at the expected rate for her age or when her weight is disproportionately low compared with her height and head circumference. In order to grow, a child must take in adequate calories, absorb those calories, and use them for growth.

If a child is not growing well, first consider whether she is actually taking in an adequate number of calories (and other nutrients). What is she being fed? How much is she offered and how often? How much does she actually take? Is she able to suck and swallow adequately? Most cases of infants failing to thrive can be solved by carefully addressing these questions.

If caloric and other nutrient intake is adequate, consider whether the calories are continuing down the gastrointestinal tract, being digested, and being absorbed into the body. Sometimes the food is vomited back up either due to a blockage in the gastrointestinal tract or to a condition called gastroesophageal reflux, in which food travels backward from the stomach to the esophagus. Sometimes the calories make it through the stomach but are not absorbed—they are lost out the other end—either because of diarrhea or because of an inability to absorb the nutrients.

When adequate calories are consumed and absorbed into the body, the calories could be spilling out in the urine, if the kidneys are not effective at holding in the protein. If the fuel remains safely in the body, the body could still be burning it at a faster-than-normal rate, leaving insufficient calories for growth.

Some children will fail to thrive, even in the face of adequate calorie absorption, simply from extreme neglect. Kids who are not hugged, held, and cared for don't grow. This has been clearly demonstrated in orphanages where the adult-child ratio is very low. Even if these children are being well nourished, they often fail to thrive simply because they lack personal care.

The most common causes for failure to thrive vary with age. In the first three months of life, feeding difficulties, infections, gastroesophageal reflux, inborn errors of metabolism, cystic fibrosis, and milk-protein intolerance top the list. Simply switching to formula is not a sufficient solution if your child doesn't respond with steady growth.

Many infants regain their birth weights by one week of age. Most regain their birth weights by two weeks of age and have a steady weight gain thereafter. A child who has gone seven weeks without regaining her birth weight deserves a thorough workup to determine the cause. This workup should begin with a detailed feeding history and a careful physical examination. If the cause for failure to thrive is not apparent, the next step is to run some simple screening lab tests, including a complete blood count (CBC).

Every mom wants to make sure that her child is growing. This instinct runs strong and deep and is there for good reason. When growth is not proceeding apace, take steps to correct the problem or to discover its cause.

GUILT *(See also Playing)*

Someday, the hubbub of having a new baby will die down and you'll get feeding and changing under control. Then what? What are you supposed to do all day long? Nowadays, when children are being prepared for future genius while they're still in the womb (or so it seems), it feels as if you should be stimulating your baby's mind all the time. An overwhelming tone that new parents sound on

Parent Soup's message boards is one of guilt: the fear of not doing enough for the baby. Seasoned parents come to the rescue.

The Problem

Q: I am a new mother with a two-month-old daughter. I love spending time with my daughter, but sometimes I feel guilty that I don't always know what to do with her. What kinds of things should I be doing to keep her interested and stimulated?

~ *Parent Soup member Kabrams701*

The Solution

A: Just hearing you say you feel guilty about not doing things with her brings back floods of memories. *Don't feel guilty!* Any time you spend with your daughter is excellent time for both of you. You don't have to entertain her, and believe me, the time will come when you will. Be close to her, talk to her, pat her. Sing and read stories. Don't let this special time be clouded by guilt.

~ *Alane J.,*
Brooklyn, New York

A: Children also need downtime and time to play, discover, and not

be entertained. If you are worrying about not doing enough, chances are you are doing plenty.

~ Suzanne L., Pasadena, California

A: Don't worry about your child not being interested in what you are doing for her. Just keep doing what you're doing—reading, playing music, and outdoor activities. They know you love them, and that is what's important. Before you know it, your child will be the one keeping you busy with her activities. Enjoy now.

~ Mindy, California

A: Don't worry about entertaining your child all the time. He will learn a lot from watching you do everyday things. You can involve him by saying, "Look, I'm putting the laundry in the washer. Here is a blue sock." Make funny faces and let him "help" sort out the clothes. Bury him under the clothes so he can easily get out, then get really excited when he does get out. In other words, do what you need to do, but get him involved. Also, try to give him some downtime. People, even young ones, need time to unwind without stimuli coming at them all the time. They also need to learn about the world, and what better way than to let them see and participate in the things you and other adults do.

~ Vanessa, Washington

HEAD BUMPS

When your little one literally hits life's road bumps head on, Dr. Greene advises that you breathe deeply and check for these symptoms.

h head bumps

DR. GREENE'S INSIGHT

Fortunately, most "bonks" are not serious. Nevertheless, when we hear the awful thud of a child's head, our breath catches, and for a moment we fear the worst. A prompt cry after the injury is reassuring. It is normal for a child to feel sleepy after hitting his head, and it is even OK for him to vomit once or twice. If your baby has any of the following conditions, however, call your physician *right away*:

- Under six months of age

- Unconscious, even briefly

- Crying for longer than 10 minutes

- Repeated vomiting

- Blood from the ears or nose

- Rapid swelling just above the ear

- Inability to walk or talk normally

- Unequal pupil size

- Severe, worsening headache

- Neck pain

- Seizures

- Severe injury (e.g., caused by car accident, long fall, baseball bat)

Your son may be fine, but you should be in touch with an expert. If your son is unable to get up by himself immediately after the head injury, don't move him. Call 911 and wait for emergency help to arrive.

    If none of these symptoms is present, it is fine to let your son sleep, as long as you wake him every half hour for the first six hours after the fall. After this, awaken your son at your bedtime and again four hours later to check on his

PARENT POLL

How long did it take you to feel confident as a parent after the birth of your first child?

Of 720 total votes

immediately—my instincts kicked right in 20.69%

a few days, then things settled down 17.63%

a few weeks to a month before I could breathe easily  36.52%

I still feel like I'm doing something wrong 25.13%

1 bowl = 100 parents

status. If at any time your child seems to develop a suspicious symptom, call your doctor.

After reading a list like this, it is tempting to try to protect your son from every situation that might result in an injury. It is appropriate to use good judgment in deciding what activities are safe for your child, but it is also important to allow him the opportunity to express himself through physical activity. Sometimes growth means taking risks, but appropriate risks are worth taking!

IMMUNIZATIONS

The decision to immunize or not to immunize has been hotly debated in pediatricians' waiting rooms around the country and at Parent Soup. In many cases, the point is moot—the state requires most of the immunizations listed in this book before the child will be allowed to enter kindergarten (although many states allow children to forgo immunization if they have a religious or medical exemption). However, it's important to remember that these immunizations were developed and required by public health officials to keep the public healthy, and some dangerous diseases such as smallpox have been eradicated through using vaccination. Dr. Greene explains how to decide whether to give your child the chickenpox vaccine, a relatively new vaccine that is a hot topic among parents on the Parent Soup message boards.

Chickenpox Vaccine

Q: I am currently trying to assess whether to vaccinate my 15-month-old and 3-year-old for chickenpox. Can you give me the pros and cons?

What are you recommending to your patients? Everyone I talk to
seems to have a different opinion.

~ *Leslie, California*

DR. GREENE'S INSIGHT

A: In deciding on any immunization, it is wise to weigh the risks versus the
benefits of the vaccine as well as the risks versus benefits of not receiving
the vaccine. Children who do not get the vaccine are likely to develop
chickenpox. This common viral infection is usually mild and not life-
threatening. Although children may be miserable with it for several days and
miss a week of school or day care (stranding parents at home), they will
likely recover from the 250 to 500 itchy blisters with nothing more to show
than a few small scars. Each year, however, about 200,000 of the millions
of people in the world who contract chickenpox become seriously ill with
complications such as pneumonia or encephalitis (inflammation of the
brain). About two thousand of these die. People who are at higher risk for
complications include those with an already weak immune system, those
with eczema or other skin conditions, adolescents, and adults.

Benefits of the Vaccine

The main benefit of the chickenpox vaccine to individuals is long-lasting
immunity to chickenpox. All other common vaccines require a booster dose
to maintain immunity. The chickenpox vaccine lasts so long that a booster
dose has not yet been recommended, although it probably will be at some
future time. To date, those who have received the vaccine have a much lower
incidence of shingles than those who actually had chickenpox. Those who
receive the vaccine also have a dramatically decreased risk of scarring.

The other major benefit of the vaccine is an economic one. The vaccine
reduces the costs related to the disease, including the costs of missed

work, school, and child care. This savings is a major force in the drive for universal immunization in the United States.

What Are the Risks of the Vaccine?

A chickenpox vaccine, developed in Japan 25 years ago, has since been given to more than two million people, with a good track record for safety. A similar vaccine has been used in the United States since the early 1980s. Reported adverse effects are generally mild: soreness, swelling, or a rash at the injection site, and fever, fatigue, or fussiness are the most common. The vaccine is not recommended for immunocompromised people or for pregnant women.

Bottom Line

While I remain unconvinced of the long-term wisdom of immunizing everyone against this generally mild disease, I believe the following people *should* get the vaccine, as the benefits outweigh the risks:

- Children with eczema (or other chronic skin conditions), asthma (or other chronic lung conditions), or a strong family history of allergic conditions

- Adolescents or adults who have not yet had chickenpox

- People living in areas where immunization is widespread (since they will have a smaller chance to gain natural immunity by being exposed to the disease)

Before the vaccine became available, my three oldest children suffered through the chickenpox. Recently, I chose to give my youngest child the chickenpox vaccine, simply because we live in an area where the

RECOMMENDED SCHEDULE FOR IMMUNIZATIONS

The Advisory Committee on Immunization Practices, a subcommittee of the American Academy of Pediatrics and the American Academy of Family Physicians, has recommended a schedule for childhood immunizations:

Hepatitis B #1	Birth
Hepatitis B #2	1 to 4 months
Hepatitis B #3	6 to 18 months
Hepatitis B #1 to 3	11 to 12 years (if not previously vaccinated)
Diphtheria, tetanus, pertussis (DTP) #1	2 months
DTP #2	4 months
DTP #3	6 months
DTP #4	12 to 18 months
DTP #5	4 to 6 years
H. influenzae type B (HIB) #1	2 months
HIB #2	4 months
HIB #3	6 months
HIB #4	12 to 15 months
Polio #1	2 months
Polio #2	4 months
Polio #3	6 to 18 months
Polio #4	4 to 6 years
Measles, mumps, and rubella (MMR) #1	12 to 15 months
MMR #2	4 to 6 years or 11 to 12 years
Varicella zoster virus vaccine (chickenpox)	12 to 18 months
Varicella zoster virus vaccine (chickenpox)	11 to 12 years (if unvaccinated and hasn't had chickenpox)

immunization is widespread and I felt it was in his best interest to be vaccinated.

MOTHER LOVE

Enough of the how-tos and wherefores of motherhood—how does it make you feel? We've all heard the expression "a face only a mother could love." Now you know what it means: no matter what your baby looks like or how he acts, you will love him. Completely. Utterly. Resoundingly, even. Some Parent Soupers have tried to express the overwhelming emotions they've experienced as mothers. As Parent Soup member Michelle Q. aptly puts it, "Being a mom is the best high in the world."

Q: I'm a new mother, and several times a day I find myself incredibly overwhelmed by the depth and power of love I feel for my daughter (now 11 weeks old). Tears well up in my eyes and I feel flooded by emotion. I just started a class and leave her with a sitter twice a week for three hours. I thought this was important because I'm afraid I'm going to end up smothering my daughter with motherliness and overprotectiveness. I thought it would get easier to be apart from her with time, but instead it gets harder. Does anyone else experience such intense emotion? I'm not going to be a sick, clingy mother who never lets her child develop independence, am I?

   ~ *Parent Soup member CCZG*

A: What you're experiencing is just plain-old mother love! My son is five and a half months, and I have left him once at three months to get my hair cut—and thought I was gonna bawl the whole time I was gone.

Once your daughter gets older, the situation will change and you'll find yourself letting go a little, just when she needs to be a little more independent.

~ *Sam S., Summit, New Jersey*

A: Oh my God! You don't know how good it makes me feel to read these posts. I thought I was going crazy!! I began to feel this overwhelming love while I was in the hospital. I boo-hooed so much every time I saw her. One night, the nurse wheeled her in, all swaddled and looking at me, and I just burst into tears because I realized I loved her so much. I'm crying now just thinking about it! That was five months ago!! It gets better though. My first three weeks were bad because I was crying over everything. I got her picture taken, and when I saw the photos, I cried my eyes out. I have never felt this much love in my life. I feel happy, sad, and vulnerable. I can deal with it a bit better now, and even though I don't cry as much, I do things like stare at her while she's sleeping, play with her feet, smell her. Being a mom is the best high in the world.

~ *Michele Q., Dana Point, California*

Mom is wow spelled upside down!

~ *Parent Soup member CJmommy*

MULTIPLES

Multiples mean multiple mouths to feed, diapers to change, and cries to be soothed, all at the same time. Of course, multiple babies also mean multiple hugs and kisses, first smiles, first words, and everything else. Here are some tips to help you deal with the logistical aspects, such as how to feed two babies at once.

Buying for Two

I now realize that I should try things out first and start with *one* of everything. We only ever use one swing at a time, but of course we bought two.

~ *Lisa S., Sutton, Massachusetts*

The one thing that I have found to be a godsend are bouncy seats. If you bottle-feed and they get hungry at the same time, just plop them in the seats on either side of you, and you can feed both at the same time. Also, if you're looking for a little "mommy time," you can put one seat under each foot and bounce them while reading a book, watching TV, or talking on the phone.

~ *Michelle K., St. Charles, Missouri*

Feeding Two at a Time

My main tip for parents of twins is a handy little thing called the Hands Free Podee bottle. It is available from Toys "R" Us. It sounds horrible, but it is a lifesaver. It is a bottle with a straw in it with a nipple attached at the end. The baby can drink from this at about one month. You don't have to hold the baby, just prop them up in the car seat or swing and put the bottle next to them. I know, I know, but those people who say you must hold your baby to bond never had twins!

~ *Christine O., White Plains, New York*

We use one spoon, one bowl, and separate bottles. Face it, they share toys, and we all know the toys go directly in their mouths. We started with separate everything, but then real life slapped us in the face and we simplified. Of course, if one is sick, the separate approach is definitely the way to go.

~ *Tamara P., Toronto, Ontario*

Multiple Blessings by Betty Rothbart, MSW, is a wonderful resource! She has all sorts of ideas on how to feed two at a time, and there are pictures!

~ *Dawn W., Byron Center, Michigan*

I would sit on the bed, Indian style, but with the soles of my feet together. Then I put a pillow over my calves and put the boys on the pillow facing me. In that position, you can hold a bottle for each one or prop the bottles on a blanket or another pillow, leaving both hands free to rub the babies' heads (or change the channel on the TV).

~ *Susan, Texas*

I sit on the sofa with one twin on either side of me. Lay them so their heads are pointed toward the edge and their feet are pointed toward the back of the sofa. If they need a little more support, you can prop them up on firm pillows or rolled-up blankets. This worked really well.

~ *Lori F., Phoenix, Arizona*

Double the Diapers, Double the Smell
I should have bought stock in Renuzit.

~ *Parent Soup member Quinntann*

Getting Around with Multiples
My sister has twins and she's getting tired of hearing, "Boy, do you have your hands full!" Every time she takes the twins out she also

gets, "You sure are brave," and "Please tell me you're baby-sitting!" She has three kids who are less than two years apart. I want to print up a T-shirt for her that says, "Yes, they are twins. Yes, they are all mine. And yes, I have my hands full. Now you owe me a nickel!" Whaddaya think?

~ *Rip W., Summit, New Jersey*

A girl in our twins group swore by slings. She wore two at a time, crossing opposite shoulders. (Yes, they overlapped slightly.) She said that this gave her both hands to prepare meals and so forth. My girls hated them and screamed every time I tried it. I'm sure it depends on the babies, their size, and your strength. I would suggest borrowing one (or two) or even trying them at the store before investing the cash.

~ *Tamara P., Toronto, Ontario*

Keeping Your Sanity

Q: Has anyone used leashes on their twins? I've learned to never say never, and this was an idea that I thought, No way. Now with the girls walking in different directions (needless to say), well, I'm considering it. I try to keep them in the stroller. But sometimes that's hard. Please help!

~ *Tamara P., Toronto, Ontario*

A: I bought leashes for my twins after my first experience in the mall. But I gave them up—I looked like an Indian tied to the stake! They spun me around and twisted me so, I didn't get

---

DR. GREENE'S INSIGHT: My mom had twins when I was two years old. She says the biggest secret to making it with three kids under three is to slightly anticipate their needs: feed them just before they get hungry; pick them up just before they get fussy. (Change their diapers just before they poop? Not!) She says that she found that each intervention took less time when she did it early.

to go into one store, and I felt I was running harder than ever before. I just stick with the stroller and try to never let them escape—or I know I am doomed.

~ *Robin, California*

We use harnesses on our 20-month-old twin boys. It's hard when you are alone, because you get tangled up. But when my husband and I take them for a walk, it really helps. I recommend them highly for safety and sanity.

~ *Parent Soup member Bhegner568*

MUST HAVES FOR NEW MOMS
(See also Penny-Pinchers)

You could go crazy (and get into some serious debt) buying for your new baby. Here's some help on navigating the baby department, with tips on products that will actually make your life easier, as well as what to avoid.

Absolute Favorites
The two best baby items I can think of are the Mommy Bear (it also comes in a Mommy Bunny) and sheet savers. The Mommy Bear is just adorable—it emits sounds of the womb to help baby sleep at night. When baby is older, you can take the sound box out, and it's still a great teddy bear. The sheet savers were a lifesaver for me—my son threw up a lot! They tie right onto the crib rails like a bumper and can be removed without taking all the sheets off, and they come in packages of two.

~ *Michelle, Maryland*

m must haves for new moms

I found the baby swing to be a real lifesaver, from the time my son was two months up to now (seven months). He would often fall asleep in the swing when other methods had failed. When he was four months, we got an Exersaucer, and he loves it! It has helped strengthen his legs tremendously; even his pediatrician was impressed. I am a first-time mom who went nuts trying to find the most useful products for our baby. One thing I strongly recommend is a good crib bumper. Most of the cute and colorful bumpers you find for sale are way too soft and cushiony, and it seems contradictory that people try to avoid pillows and soft bedding in the crib, just to put those kinds of bumpers in there. The one I bought (thanks to my sister-in-law's advice) is very square and covered by strong vinyl. It is soft enough to absorb baby's bumps but not to sink.

~ *Patrizia J., Gordonsville, Virginia*

> **DR. GREENE'S INSIGHT:** Babies with good head control can enjoy the swing as early as three weeks—the beginning of colic.

What to Avoid

I found the wipe warmer to be a waste—warm wipes crumble in your hand. Try to wait on spending major money until after the baby is born. We have more useless baby stuff. It is amazing what you *don't* need.

~ *Charis P., Maitland, Florida*

I would not spend a lot of money on a cradle, unless you're planning on a big family, because the baby won't stay in it long—they grow too fast! I would get a stroller with cloth padding (softer).

~ *Parent Soup member NerakMost*

A Clothes Call

I want to save all you new moms out there from making the tragic mistake that I already made. Keep your little girls out of those darling long nightgowns that are so tempting because they look so darn cute! I put my daughter in one, and as she was toddling toward us, she tripped on the hem, got her foot caught, and twisted her leg, resulting in a fractured femur: eight weeks in a cast from the waist down for the poor little thing, not to mention our having to deal with Social Services. I learned the hard way that cute is nice, but settle for practical.

~ *Carla, Maryland*

Things to Have Ready When You
Get Home from the Hospital
- Infant Tylenol (or Pediacare or Motrin).
  I even give these as presents after I had to run out at 4 A.M. to get Tylenol when my son was two weeks old.

- Bulb syringe or aspirator (things that clean out the nose)

- Bottle bags

- Humidifier

- Diapers (of course)
  ~ *Parent Soup member LoriDeCa*

DR. GREENE'S INSIGHT: Holding your tired eyes open at four in the morning, concerned for a fussy child, is no fun. You want to give the child anything that will help him feel better. Still, I don't recommend giving Tylenol to children under two months old without talking to a doctor first [see Fever]. I also wouldn't use Pediacare or Motrin with babies less than six months old without clearing it with your pediatrician first.

These medicines behave very differently in very young children. Also, mild illnesses and serious illnesses in the first eight weeks can look similar. If your newborn seems sick, at least call your doctor before administering medicine at home.

Prepare a basket for your time at home in the beginning. Put some barf towels, your baby book, a notebook and pen for lists (logging your baby's functions and feeding, doctor numbers, etc.), a cordless phone, some snacks for you, and a big jug of water with ice in it. Get a bunch of

blankets, onesies, and jammies. Don't go overboard on outfits, because
he won't need them at first, and he'll be much more comfy in jammies.
Stick to terry cloth; it breathes. Buy a good monitor! And post the
number of your favorite takeout restaurant everywhere!

~ *Cary O., Woodbridge, Virginia*

The Basics
My sister just had a baby and I've been helping her out. Here's what we
found is good to have on hand: diapers, lotion, bath stuff (at first you
may want to get a large sponge made especially for newborns), your
camera and film, a diaper pail, a bouncy seat, some music, a mobile,
wipes, and crib pads so you don't have to change the sheets every day.
A baby book and a baby's-first-year calendar are great things if you can
afford them. Add a do-not-disturb sign for the front door when those
unwanted guests arrive at nap time.

~ *Erika F., Golf, Illinois*

The things I have found most useful are NUK pacifiers, onesies, infant
gowns (so much easier for diaper-changing those first six to eight weeks),
bottles (even if breastfeeding, situations arise when a bottle is needed), at
least 12 cloth diapers (tons of uses), a drying rack for bottles, nipples, a
baby swing, and a Snugli or sling. Here's more for your list—a vaporizer,
diaper disposal bags, sterile saline drops (helps with stuffy noses), and
Dove or Camay bath soap. At our hospital, we recommend using these
brands at first instead of baby soaps because they are less drying to the
skin. Also add crib pads that protect the sheets.

~ *Rebecca, Virginia*

After having two kids, I've got some suggestions on what to get or not to get. First, don't get everything in newborn sizes—you'd be surprised how fast they reach 11 pounds. I had quite a few gowns instead of sleepers; they fit longer and make middle-of-the-night changes easier. But the ones with elastic at the bottom and the string-closing ones get tangled on little toes. Onesies are great—I use them year-round, in summer as sleepers and in winter for warmth. As far as sleepers, try to get the basic ones, without buttons and bows (my daughter loved to chew on these). Resale shops are great places to look for infant clothes— babies grow too fast to ruin an outfit. You can also sometimes find swings and bouncy seats there. I have about 20 receiving blankets, and I actually use them. I put one over rubberized things to keep leaks from getting on the sheets—it's softer and sometimes soaks up the whole leak. My kids like to cuddle with them. And I layer them instead of using a bulky comforter. I recommend three or four sheets; you'd be surprised how often you change them.

~ *Alexia W., South Lyon, Michigan*

Get lots of gowns (wonderful at night), receiving blankets, and onesies. My son lived in these the first couple of months. Burp cloths or cloth diapers are good to have for spit ups. Buy several sheets, a couple of waterproof mattress pads, and also a soft, fleecy blanket for cold weather, a couple of caps, and some socks. Don't go overboard stocking up on newborn diapers—wait to see how big your baby is (they outgrow them quickly). Have a thermometer on hand if your hospital doesn't provide you with one.

~ *Parent Soup member FSUkitty*

I found a swing to be our most-used item so far. Our son loves his and takes all his naps in it. Alcohol and cotton balls are good for the umbilical area, and petroleum jelly and gauze if needed for a circumcision. Get hooded bath towels, washcloths, and a baby tub. We also used a cradle the first few months in our room, so that taking care of him at night would be easier.

~ *Carol N., Rialto, California*

PACIFIERS *(See also Thumb Sucking)*

Babies suck to comfort themselves. They also suck to eat, so sometimes it's hard to tell if they need to be fed or if they need to be comforted. But if the only nipple you offer (whether it's real or artificial) dispenses food, you run the risk of overfeeding your baby. That's why pacifiers can be your best friend for a time. They also have a downside: children can come to rely on them well beyond the age when they need to suck for comfort, and pacifiers can even help transmit ear infections (see Dr. Greene's comments on pages 150–151). So, as with all things, moderation is best.

How Pacifiers Can Work for You

I did not give my daughter a pacifier when she cried all the time because I had the impression they were bad. So what did I do? I nursed her, thinking she was hungry. Then she would spit up and I kept thinking it must be me or my milk or something I was doing wrong. I kept taking her to the doctor, but they never found anything wrong. So I switched to formula. It still didn't help. One day I broke down and gave her a

pacifier and she was fine. Apparently all she needed to do was suck!
When I was nursing her constantly, she would be up the whole night. As
soon as we gave her a pacifier, she slept.

~ *Amber H., Savannah, Georgia*

PARENT POLL

When should a child stop using a pacifier?

Of 1,396 total votes

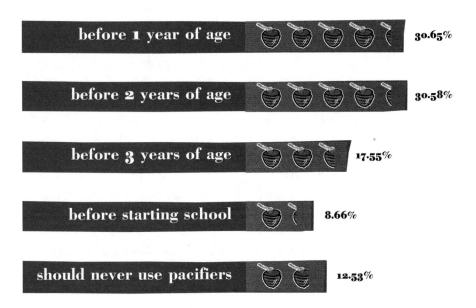

before **1** year of age — 30.65%

before **2** years of age — 30.58%

before **3** years of age — 17.55%

before starting school — 8.66%

should never use pacifiers — 12.53%

1 bowl = 100 parents

p   pacifiers

Better than Prozac??

I wish I could calm down with such a simple thing as a pacifier. Wouldn't it be great to come home and unwind in a hot bath with a pacifier? I have to admit, though, that when my newborn daughter took to one so completely, it unnerved me. However, she is now using it less frequently (at two and a half months), mainly after her bottle when she needs extra sucking or when she has been through something stressful, such as a bath or an intense session of playing. As soon as she gets the pacifier, she can focus on calming down and often discards it after she is calm. Don't worry—nobody makes it to high school sucking on a pacifier!

~ *Tracey S., Denver, Colorado*

Wean When They're Too Young to Ask for It Back

My son used one for the first 10 months, and finally I decided to take it away from him because I was afraid he would become addicted to it. At that age, they are too young to ask for another one, and he never really knew the difference after the first two days without it.

~ *Melanie L., Raleigh, North Carolina*

DR. GREENE'S INSIGHT

University researchers from Finland have recently published a study of 845 children attending day care. They followed the children for 15 months, keeping track of behaviors that might influence the number of ear infections. These included breastfeeding, parental smoking, thumb sucking, bottle use, and social class.

To their surprise, they found that the strongest association was with pacifier use, which increased the frequency of ear infections by 50 percent. Presumably, either the sucking motion associated with pacifier use hinders proper eustachian tube functioning (which normally keeps the middle ear open and clean) or—particularly in day care—the pacifiers act as fomites (germ-covered objects that spread infection). The authors suggest that pacifiers be used only during the first 10 months of life when the need for sucking is strongest.

I believe that sucking is an important comfort measure for many babies. Moreover, sucking objects of various types have been used in most cultures throughout history. In my opinion, this study suggests two take-home lessons:

1. If your child is plagued by frequent ear infections, stopping the use of a pacifier is worth a try—certainly before prophylactic antibiotics or surgery.

2. For any child, it is prudent to wean the pacifier as soon as it is no longer something that the child actively needs.

How to Wean a Child off a Pacifier

Too often, pacifier use persists into middle childhood either out of habit or because the pacifier has become the child's "lovey," not from any true need to suck. If this is the case for your child, here are some tips that will help you wean him or her in a constructive way from pacifier use. First, restrict pacifier use to sleep time and stressful situations (getting shots), since most children will become less attached as they experience more of the day without the pacifier. Then make the pacifiers less attractive, while at the same time introducing a new comfort object. To make the pacifiers less attractive, you might put on one drop of "bitter apple" (found in pet stores), giving the pacifier a mildly unpleasant taste. Combination teddy bear and blankets, such as those made by Dakin, make a nice alternative for comforting. With most kids it is easier to deal with the pacifier issue at a young age rather than waiting until they become more attached and the habit becomes more ingrained.

PENNY-PINCHERS

It sure is easy to drop loads of money on your new baby, what with the latest toys and adorable (but expensive) baby clothes, not to mention doctor visits, diapers, food, and on and on. But you don't have to break the bank to have a happy, healthy baby. There are many ways to save money here and there. Parent Soup member Lori K. probably says it best when she notes that the most important thing to have in trying to cut back on needless expenses is creativity. "The ideas are endless," she adds, "if you let your imagination do the work, rather than your pocketbook." Here are some ideas to jump-start your imagination.

Decorating Made Cheap and Easy

When I was looking to decorate my daughter's nursery, I couldn't find anything I liked on the market, so I did the following: I wanted a Dr. Seuss theme, so I took several Seuss books to the library and copied them onto transparent film. Then I used an overhead projector and projected the pictures on the wall in her room. I traced the images with a pencil and used acrylics to paint between the lines, with a black magic marker to do the outlining. Trust me, I'm no artist and it was so easy!

~ Honor C., Knoxville, Tennessee

Forgo the Bassinet

I never used a bassinet for my two kids; instead I purchased a portacrib. That was the best investment—a baby doesn't outgrow it as fast, and it's great for a playpen, too. It's also perfect for traveling.

~ Laurie P., Hoboken, New Jersey

For Swing Lovers
If you use a battery-operated swing, invest in some rechargeable batteries and a charger. It saved us a lot of money!
~ *Susie L., Kingsport, Tennessee*

Getting Used to Buying Used
I consider myself an experienced penny-pincher. With my staying at home with four children, it's become my home "business." One of the first and foremost rules of penny-pinching is don't buy something new unless you absolutely have to. Many people have a revulsion for used items, but I figure that, if I buy it new and use it once, it's used! You can find great used clothing, furniture, appliances, toys, books, and more at garage sales, consignment shops, thrift stores, and the like.
~ *Lori K., Harrisburg, Missouri*

We have recently started combing the consignment sales for clothes for the baby. It's amazing to buy Little Me, Baby Gap, and Gymboree things that have hardly been worn and spending about $5 to $10 instead of $28 to $40!
~ *Elizabeth F., Brentwood, Tennessee*

Cooking Up Savings
I almost never use coupons. Haven't yet seen a coupon for whole-wheat flour or carrots. Why waste money on Hamburger Helper? Or sugary cereals that are really candy anyway? Cook from scratch! It's the only way to get cheap and nutritious food. It tastes better, too. An excellent cookbook for beginners is *Whole Foods for the Whole Family*. It tells you how to make everything from scratch—and that doesn't take as much

time as you might think. I can make real cheese sauce for pasta in only a few minutes. It still takes just as long to heat the water and cook the pasta, whether or not you use a box. So you're not saving any time by putting little packets of fake cheese powder onto your macaroni. You may think that the amount of money you save by never buying convenience foods and new clothing isn't worth it, but it is. Add it up, and those little changes together become thousands of dollars! Little things really do mean a lot.

~ *Michelle H., Concord, Illinois*

Homemade Finger Paint

¼ cup cornstarch

2 cups cold water

Food coloring

Mix ingredients in a saucepan. Boil until the mixture thickens. Cool and pour into containers. I usually double this recipe, omitting the food coloring, and pour it into several jars. Then I add the food coloring.

~ *Cathy B., Chicago, Illinois*

When I was working with one-year-olds at a day-care center, I tried out a fun activity that I read about on this message board. Add liquid soap to finger paint—that way it doesn't stain clothes and it washes off very easily. Then you have each child make handprints on a piece of thin cloth and paint stems and leaves on each one to make little flower hands. It's really sweet and the parents *love* them.

~ *Amy R., Aiken, South Carolina*

Make Your Own Diaper Wipes

Save loads of money on diaper wipes by making your own. You need a half roll of Bounty paper towels, 1½ cups water, 2 tablespoons of baby bath, and a container.

1. Put paper towels in a container.

2. Mix water and baby bath.

3. Pour mixture over the paper towels.

4. Wait one minute and then remove cardboard roll. Pull wipes from center. Keep the container covered.

~ *Renee G., Redstone Arsenal, Alabama*

When I make baby wipes, I use Job Squad paper towels. They are more expensive than Bounty (and much sturdier) but still way cheaper than regular wipes. I also add a little bit of baby oil to the wipes.

~ *Kelly E., Winter Springs, Florida*

PICKY EATERS *(See also Solids)*

As frustrating as it may be, you can't force a baby to eat. And you can't reason with a baby. So what do you do when your child isn't eating enough of the things that will make him grow and be healthy? You can always make funny noises and act like an airplane trying to get them to open their mouths and swallow some nourishment.

p picky eaters

If you need some new material, see "Going for an Academy Award" below. And for some solid common sense on how kids eat, see the rest of the Parent Soup member posts listed in this section.

Try to Relax

I have a picky eater. One thing I've learned is they sense your unease. Try to relax about what they eat. If your child is still getting breast milk or formula and growing appropriately, she's doing fine.

~ *Anne W., Cranford, New Jersey*

Going for an Academy Award

The thing a kid trying new foods needs most is reactions. Kids *love* reactions. So sit the baby at the table, and the minute some food goes into his or her mouth, get this amazed look on your face, as if you've just seen people from another planet. Get it from time to time, so they don't know when to expect it. If the child finishes what's on the plate, pretend to fall out of your chair in shock. It works!

~ *Doug F., Canton, Ohio*

Let Your Child Find Her Own Eating Style

My daughter has always been small, but she thrived on breast milk until she entered day care. A high-needs baby, she didn't get enough attention in day care and ate very little while she was there. She didn't gain any weight between six and eight months. I quit my job to stay home with her, and she was tested for all kinds of illness. It turns out she is just a picky eater. First of all, we started supplementing with Toddler's Best, the only formula she would drink. We found she far preferred to feed herself. We fixed sampler plates with little bits of different finger foods. We learned she will never eat the same thing the next day and never very much of any one thing. And everything looks better if it comes off my plate. One of the hardest things for me to give up was the idea of her eating only pure, healthy foods. (Some of her favorite foods are Goldfish, Top Ramen, macaroni and cheese, fish sticks, and Tater Tots.) But now, the main thing I worry about is that she is healthy and thriving.

> DR. GREENE'S INSIGHT: For most kids, even most picky eaters, it's much better to relax than to try to push food. The more you push, the more kids will resist!

~ *Janet S., Raleigh, North Carolina*

Many children are grazers. They prefer to have many small meals, rather than three formal ones. On a little table I leave out dry Cheerios, raisins, a cup of juice, and crackers and let my toddler get a snack when he wants it. As long as he eats, I don't really care when.

~ *Michelle J., Fairfield, Connecticut*

PIMPLES

You're probably thinking, "Isn't it a little early?" Nope. Those little red bumps on your newborn's otherwise beautiful skin are probably pimples.

DR. GREENE'S INSIGHT

When a beautiful newborn's face breaks out with red bumps, it's called baby acne. It tends to occur at about the same age as the baby's peak gas production and fussiness. How attractive! Parents are often quite concerned about how these bumps look and about their significance.

Not to worry—the bumps are more than likely nothing more than fleeting evidence of the connection between a mother and her baby. During the final moments of pregnancy, adult female hormones cross the placenta to enter her baby's bloodstream. Among other things (such as maturing his lungs), this influx stimulates the oil glands on baby's skin, eventually giving rise to baby acne.

Fleshy or red pimples can be present at birth, but typically they appear at three to four weeks of age. They occur predominantly on the cheeks, but they are also quite common on the forehead and chin. Whiteheads are sometimes present. This condition tends to come and go until the baby is between four and six months old.

The acne will be most prominent when your baby is hot or fussy (increased blood flow to the skin) or when his skin is irritated. If his skin comes into contact with cloth laundered in harsh detergents, or if it becomes wet from saliva or milk that he has spit up, the condition may appear worse for several days.

Gently cleanse his face once a day with water and perhaps a mild baby soap. Oils and lotions do not help and may aggravate the condition. If the acne is severe or lasts beyond six months, your pediatrician may prescribe a mild medicine to help. Otherwise you can expect that the rash will soon fade on its own.

PLAYING (See also Guilt)

Growth and development are a baby's two main objectives. And playing can help fulfill both these goals. How can you guide your baby's play to keep her happy and healthy? It can be hard for adults to jump back into the mind-set of playtime. Just in case you've forgotten, playing is not only important but also fun! Dr. Greene has some wonderful insight on how a baby's play mirrors her development. And the parents of Parent Soup have great ideas on what to do during playtime.

DR. GREENE'S INSIGHT

I encourage you to provide your child with a rich, nurturing environment in which to grow and thrive rather than directly *stimulating* your child (by doing things to her or for her). Young children tend to enjoy the moments that support their drive to grow and develop. Notice what makes your child smile or laugh. When children look into your eyes and smile, they are learning about social interactions. In this period, time with your face close at hand is one of the best gifts you can give your children.

Observe your child's spontaneous play. Children delight in activities that are in the zone of their current development. If the game is too easy, the children quickly grow bored and act out (throwing the toy across the room). If the game is too difficult, children become frustrated and lose interest. Moderately challenging activities that are moderately new engage children's interest and are often repeated again and again. You will see your children's good feelings and sense of accomplishment as they master new skills through play.

Your children's choices give you a window into their inner world. When they dissolve in delight at peekaboo, they are learning about separation and return, learning to think about objects (and people) that are not immediately present. As they enjoy putting objects into containers, they also are getting a grasp of basic physics and the nature of space and matter.

Children thrive when each day their loving environment includes just a few new experiences or people or objects. Choose these to coincide with the skills your children are working on (which you can see by observing their play). Watch for fussiness as a sign of overstimulation or boredom. When children master a task, let them wallow in their successes by repeating it over and over to increase their sense of competency. When the glow begins to fade, alter the game slightly, to make it just a bit more challenging.

Don't try to indoctrinate or force-feed learning to your children. Trust that their inner drives to learn will propel them, if interesting play is available. Conscious playing with your child will be one of the great joys of life (and great learning experiences) for both of you!

Remembering Rhymes

I highly recommend Elaine Martin's book *Baby Games*. Not only does it have the words to many, many lullabies and other songs, but it also has some fabulous ideas for playing with your baby at various stages or ages. You should also look into a CD or cassette of children's music. I have Sharon, Lois & Bram's *Mainly Mother Goose*. My son and I listen to it a couple of times a day. He loves it. We play together on the floor, while I sing or talk along to the songs and rhymes. Even though he is playing and doing other things, he is really listening. Believe me, after a few days you will know the words to so many of those old nursery rhymes that you have forgotten.

~ *Teresa C., Pittsburgh, Pennsylvania*

Go with What Works

When my daughter was one to two months old, nothing really entertained her except being in her baby swing. It got to the point where I felt guilty about having her in the swing so much. I would take her out because I felt bad that I wasn't holding her. She would howl until I put her back! I would ask my husband, "Do you think she's lonely?" "Do you think she thinks we've abandoned her?"

He finally said, "If she were unhappy, I figure she'd be crying, right?" Well, that made sense to me! So now I say, "Hey, whatever works." Now that she's three and a half months old, she spends less and less time in the swing, since she can now lie on her stomach, look around, and move a bit.

~ *Parent Soup member Jamie97735*

Easy Activities for Babies Who Are into Everything
When my daughter was eight months old, I bought her wooden blocks. I built them up into a pyramid, and then would let her knock them down. It was a lot of work on my part, but it kept her entertained. Another thing my daughter loved is my Tupperware drawer. I just let her loose in that, and she loved it!

~ *Kimberly S., New Brighton, Pennsylvania*

When my daughter was eight months old, she just would not sit still! And who can blame her, when there are so many new things to see and do and so much to explore. Something that kept her happy and in one place was Tupperware. In fact, I would allow her to open up the kitchen cabinet and take the things out herself. She loved this, and it kept her content while I did dishes.

She loved anything that grown-ups use, so I saved a few empty soda bottles and milk jugs with screw-close caps. I put a penny inside—she loved the noise that it made when she shook it. She also loved pulling things out of her diaper bag, so I took an empty gym bag with lots of zipper

> **DR. GREENE'S INSIGHT:** Be careful, though! Pennies can be a choking hazard.

compartments and filled it with toys. She had a blast pulling everything out!

~ *Tracy G., Allentown, Pennsylvania*

When Art Projects Take a Toll on Your Wall

Q: My 13-month-old daughter, Christina, has recently created her first work of art. I'd like to cherish it forever, but I can't put it in a scrapbook since she made this creation on my living room wall! Does anyone know how to get crayon marks off the wall?

~ *Linda Z., Larchmont, New York*

A: My mom suggested putting a small frame around it.

~ *Chelsea S., Spring Hill, Tennessee*

A: Here are two ways to get it off. A product called Goof Off is available at hardware stores, and it gets anything off—stickers, crayons, ink, markers, chewing gum. The second is a little more time-consuming and not guaranteed. Warm up your iron on a low-medium setting and take a white cotton cloth (cloth diapers work great) and iron over the crayon marks. Put the cloth over the spot and iron, then fold and iron some more. Keep at it until it's gone. Before you get to work, you can put a piece of white paper on the wall and iron it so you will have a print of the picture.

~ *Tarrant F., Eugene, Oregon*

A: I found that a little WD-40 works wonders at taking crayon off the walls. But now we only have the washable crayons in our house.

~ *Christine O., White Plains, New York*

How About Swimming Lessons?

Q: Our Red Cross offers swim lessons for babies six months and older. I thought it might be a good way to get our daughter used to the water and something fun for us to do together. Has anyone else done this?

    ~ Leslie K., Las Cruces, New Mexico

A: I started my daughter in swim lessons at 14 months and my son at 6½ months. Both love them—not only is it great for getting them used to the water, but it is wonderful mommy-child time. I would recommend swim lessons to anyone who's interested.

    ~ Anne B., Auburn, Washington

A: We had a great time at swim lessons, although my son was a little bit older. It was a great place to meet other parents and learn bath and swimming games.

    ~ Tarrant F., Eugene, Oregon

A: I know a child's swim teacher who says not to take children under one year to swim lessons because of chilling and skin irritation from chlorine, so be sure to see that your baby is warm enough and isn't bothered in any way from being in the pool.

    ~ Susan H., Syracuse, New York

Songs and Rhymes

One of my favorite song-games is silly. It goes like this:

    The grand old Duke of York, he had ten thousand men.

    He marched them up to the top of the hill

    And he marched them down again.

    And when they're up, they're up

TRIVIA QUESTION

At what age does a baby see as well as an adult?

a. Two days after birth

b. Four months

c. One year

d. Three years

e. Ten years

Answer: b

So don't expect baby to see all those mobiles and nursery decorations for a while!

From *Parent Soup: The Game*

163

And when they're down, they're down

And when they're only half-way up

They're neither up nor down.

You can sit on the floor with your legs bent and put the baby on your knees and move your legs up and down at the appropriate parts of the song.

~ *Leah C., Silver Spring, Maryland*

My little cousin taught me a song called "Tony Chestnut." I touch each part of the baby when I sing it (by the way, contrary to what my husband says, "nut" is your head!). "Toe-Knee-Chest-Nut, how I love you, how I love you!" My six-month-old really laughs when we sing it.

~ *Susie L., Kingsport, Tennessee*

Here's a cute little song I sing to my almost 10-week-old baby girl. Although she has no idea what I'm singing, she loves hearing mommy's voice and seeing the faces I make, and she smiles and laughs and babbles along with me:

Five little monkeys jumping on the bed,

One fell off and bumped its head.

Mama called the doctor, and the doctor said,

No more monkeys jumping on the bed!

Then count down with 4, 3, 2, 1 monkeys.

~ *Parent Soup member NiteKryme*

POSTPARTUM DEPRESSION

When we polled Parent Soup parents to ask, "Did you or your spouse have postpartum depression?" we found out that 66 percent of new mothers experienced some sort of "baby blues." (See page 169 for official poll results.) So if you've been feeling less exhilarated about being a parent than you expected, you are not alone. Some Parent Soup members share their tips on beating the blues, and Dr. Greene explains how to tell if what you're experiencing is a funk (which you can weather with a little support from your family and friends) or depression (which you should talk to your doctor about).

Easy Does It

Hormonal changes can cause postpartum depression (been there!), which can definitely linger for months. It's more than just the baby blues. And it's incredible how much that interrupted sleep affects you. My first child was up every two hours until she was two! My newest lets me sleep four hours at a time, and I thank my lucky stars! The combination of hormones and lack of sleep can really gang up on you. Just take one thing at a time. Yesterday I cleaned the bathrooms. Today I did the kitchen. Be sure to stay involved in activities outside the home (church, coffee with friends, co-op preschool), and always wear that makeup stuff. It can really help the ego, even overweight egos!

   ~ *Linda O., New York, New York*

Don't Be Afraid to Get Help

I went through postpartum depression when my baby hit four months. The first thing you have to do is get over the guilt and shame. Call a doctor right away. It's brought on by hormones, stress, and lack of sleep. You can be given short-term medication to help relieve it. You need to talk to someone and realize that you are doing a good job with your baby. And then focus on taking care of yourself as well as the baby.

   ~ *Kelly T., Charlestown, Rhode Island*

Personally, the biggest mistake I made was not asking for help. I know it's hard, but consider this: a mom going through postpartum depression said to me, "I didn't want anyone else to take care of my baby. Then I found myself screaming and yelling at him all the time. I figured a stranger could do better (for a short time)." Don't let it get to this point!

~ *Cindy J., Eugene, Oregon*

Is It the Blues, or Is It Depression?

Q: My wife and I have a beautiful new baby girl. We were both excited about having her (we were infertility patients). Now that she is here, my wife is miserable. She cries all the time, and I am at my wit's end. I find myself feeling angry, which I don't want to be. Is this postpartum blues? What should I do?

~ *Ron, Tennessee*

DR. GREENE'S INSIGHT

A: Parenthood often begins with a period of feeling blue. Women's bodies are the scenes of powerful tides of changing hormones in the days and weeks after a baby is born. The rising hormone levels that gradually brought about the incredible changes in your wife's body when she was carrying your daughter have now precipitously dropped.

Most new mothers (as many as 90 percent) will have periods of weepiness, mood swings, anxiety, unhappiness, and regret. Usually they last for a few days or less and are quickly forgotten. It's not unusual, however, for the blue period to come and go for six weeks. For some moms, the blues don't begin until the baby stops nursing (another time of major hormonal shifts). Hormones, however, are not the entire story. Moms who have adopted their babies also commonly go through a blue period. And many dads (though less weepy) go through a blue period of feeling unhappy, insecure, left out, and moody.

A major reason is that every new beginning is also an ending of what was before. When a baby is born, the world will never be the same. It's OK to grieve for the loss of the way life was before. Your wife no longer has the control of her own time the way she once did. Perhaps she also misses the challenges and rewards of her work. Hobbies may have been put on hold for a while. Her romance with you is also now different—it's no longer just the two of you. She may also be mourning the special intimacy of feeling her daughter inside her. Many new moms describe feeling empty inside. Also, when your wife was pregnant, complete strangers would beam at her, want to pat her tummy, and tell her she was glowing. Now your daughter is the focus of attention, and your wife—who would probably benefit more now from encouragement and practical aid—is less likely to get it. She may also be mourning the loss of her ideal figure: she may still look pregnant. When my youngest child was one month old, a door-to-door saleswoman greeted my wife and asked when the baby was due. (Needless to say, no sale!) Wearing maternity clothes when pregnancy is over just isn't fun, but usually nothing else is comfortable yet.

Now add sleep deprivation to all this. Your wife is probably more exhausted than she has ever been. Whenever people are sleep deprived, they are more subject to swings of emotion and to feelings of inadequacy. This, by itself, is enough to cause a blue period (ask any pediatrician). Research has shown that women with the postpartum blues tend to have babies who cry significantly more than infants of moms without depression. It hasn't been proved whether the fussy, crying babies make moms sadder, or whether the sad moms make the babies less happy—but it seems to me that both are true, and that the crying is a vicious cycle.

On a happier note, there are several things you can do to improve the situation:

- Help your wife get as much sleep as possible. Encourage her to take a nap.

- Give your daughter some bottle-feedings (of pumped breast milk, if your wife is breastfeeding). This will give your wife a break and also be a special time for you.

- Get your wife out of the house. Even brief breaks (especially time the two of you can spend together) can be very restoring, particularly if you get outside.

- Surprise your wife with your thoughtfulness. Whatever is special to your beloved, go out of your way to make it happen.

- Relieve your wife of as many of her usual roles and responsibilities as possible. Unless she genuinely wants to (and her doctor OK's it), she shouldn't have to cook, do dishes, write thank-you notes, make love, take out the trash, feed the dog, deal with her in-laws, or anything else except take care of the baby and of herself. If you are not fortunate enough to have paternity leave, it may be difficult for you to pick up all these extra household tasks. (Even if you do have paternity leave, you may be so sleep deprived yourself that you can't do them all!) If that's the case, get help from someone whom your wife trusts and finds relaxing to have around your home. At the same time, help your wife to realize that she is not marginal to the household. She is an incredibly important person!

- Get as involved as possible in caring for your baby. Ask your wife specifically what she would find most helpful. Would she like you to change more diapers? Read baby-care books? Call your pediatrician with questions? Rock the baby to sleep? Run out and buy supplies? There is almost nothing that most new mothers appreciate more from the father than concrete, loving assistance in caring for their baby.

- Shower your wife with praise and encouragement. Point out to her the things that she is doing well, the ways that she is becoming more adept at baby care, and the magnificence of what her body has done in creating a new life. Let her know that you believe in her capacity to be a wonderful mother. Gently remind her that it's normal and fine for motherhood to be an unfolding process. She doesn't have to have all the answers. Over time she will be amazed at how skilled she will become in understanding and nurturing her child.

If your wife can't sleep (even when the baby's asleep), if she doesn't want to eat, if she loses interest in life or feels hopeless, if she is having disturbing or suicidal thoughts, or if the blues are lasting more than a week or two, this might be more than postpartum blues: she might have true postpartum depression. Seek professional advice right away. Her obstetrician or family doctor is a good place to start. Don't let anyone brush this off. True depression is much less common than the blues, but when it happens, professional treatment is important and quickly

PARENT POLL

Did you or your spouse have postpartum depression?

Of 789 total votes

no   33%

yes   31%

maybe*   35%

*never got diagnosed but felt emotionally out of sorts

1 bowl = 100 parents

effective. Whether your wife's situation is the blues or full-blown depression, don't minimize it.

The weeks following your child's birth differ from any other time in your life. They are rich, complex, and often out of control. So take a deep breath. Relax. Pamper yourselves. Enjoy the little things. When life seems particularly hard, take comfort in knowing that this time will soon be over. Though life will never be the way it was before your daughter was born, soon things will settle down. In the meantime, remind yourself and your wife that this is a once-in-a-lifetime experience that you don't want to miss.

REFLUX
(See also Pacifiers, Thumb Sucking)

Many babies are born spitter-uppers. The good news is that most causes of spitting up correct themselves by one year. Still, that's a year chock full of laundry, not to mention discomfort for your little one. Although time is often the only real cure for a baby who has trouble keeping food down, many methods will help keep food down and baby happy.

Proven Spit-Up Relievers

My seven-month-old has severe reflux, and the following has helped us. For sleep positioning, try to get the baby to sleep on his side, and do not lay the baby down for at least 20 minutes after feeding! Raising the head of the crib slightly should also help. I always carry spare clothes, burp rags, and an extra blanket or two for those really messy episodes. Feeding him solids has also seemed to help. And keep in mind that 80 to 90 percent of reflux resolves itself by one year.

~ Sarah P., Flushing, Michigan

You might try burping after every ounce or half ounce while feeding (if you are bottle-feeding). And putting baby in a swing or an infant seat after feeding is a great way to ensure that they stay upright for 20 minutes. But by far the biggest improvement for us was when we switched to the silicone, NUK orthodontic nipples and Healthflow bent bottles. It was a pain to get them lined up correctly, but they really helped my son's big spit ups.

~ *Suzanne L., Pasadena, California*

Try different nipples until you find one that doesn't make baby spit up as much. Our daughter did best on the three-hole Gerber nipples. They fit most bottles.

~ *Cynthia R., Middletown, Delaware*

Make sure you're not overfeeding your baby—that'll definitely cause it all to come back up. Don't confuse the need to suck with true hunger.

~ *Kelly E., Winter Springs, Florida*

Advice from La Leche League
It can be very confusing to a mother when the baby seems to act hungry all the time. Let me assure you that babies nurse for comfort as well as for nutrition, and each child comes with a different level of "sucking need." Your baby may need extra sucking time at an "empty" breast. If you find your baby spitting up a lot, you may want to try offering only one side at each feeding and see if that works out better for him and you. At first you may end up feeding more frequently this way (because the volume of milk at each feed may be lower), but he may end up getting more satisfaction from the breast this way—and cut down on the spitting up.

r reflux

Middle-of-the-Night Time-Saver
Here's an idea to save time during middle-of-the-night spit ups: make up your baby's crib with multiple bottom sheets and a waterproof pad between each layer. If the child gets sick, you just rip off the top layer, leaving clean sheets underneath. Big help at 3 A.M.!
~ *Susan, Texas*

Stain Buster
To wipe out spit-up stains, keep a squirt bottle containing half a cup of baking soda mixed with half a cup of water. Just squirt and blot with a paper towel to neutralize spit-up odor and stains.
~ *Noni B., Lafayette, Louisiana*

Can Medication Relieve Reflux?
Q: Our pediatrician prescribed Propulsid and Zantac for a case of infant reflux. My baby is only six weeks old. I'm concerned about any possible side effects. Is this a common prescription for infants diagnosed with reflux? Are there other, alternative treatments?
~ *Hamoon, Maryland*

DR. GREENE'S INSIGHT

A: If you've ever experienced heartburn or acid indigestion, you are familiar with the dull, burning ache produced when acid sloshes up out of the stomach into the esophagus. This sloshing is called gastroesophageal reflux.

Babyhood is a time of spitting up. Since the sphincter at the top of the stomach is often loose, many babies spit up milk out of their mouths or noses. In otherwise healthy, happy babies who are growing well, the spit up is mostly milk, rather than stomach acid, and nothing needs to be done (except a lot of laundry!).

In some babies, though, the acid makes the lining of the esophagus tender, red, and swollen. The infants might arch their backs in pain. They are also at risk for inhaling the acid into the lungs, irritating their sensitive linings. These children might not gain weight well or might cry from discomfort. Some might develop a chronic cough, wheezing, or recurrent pneumonia. A few even stop breathing to try to protect their lungs.

Today the most common medicines used for reflux in babies are the two being used to treat your baby: Propulsid (cisapride) and Zantac (ranitidine, the common adult medicine for peptic ulcer). They have brought needed relief to many babies. They appear to be both effective and relatively safe. Propulsid increases the normal contractions of the stomach wall, lessening the amount of time that food remains in the stomach. Zantac blocks the production of stomach acid. These are both strong drugs.

Both drugs seem to be tolerated well by most children. The most common side effects reported from Propulsid (in those old enough to talk) are headache, diarrhea, abdominal pain, and nausea. About 6 percent of adults using Propulsid stop taking it because of side effects (compared with 3 percent who stop taking placebo because of perceived side effects). From Zantac, headaches (sometimes severe) top the list, followed by liver problems. In two studies, more than 15 percent of adults taking Zantac had temporary, reversible liver damage—at least doubling the normal death rate of liver cells while on the drug (*Physician's Desk Reference* and *Medical Economics,* 1997).

Propulsid is now known to have potentially fatal interactions with other medications. Someone taking Propulsid should *not* be given the antibiotics erythromycin, Pediazole, or Biaxin (clarithromycin). Most antifungal or

r resources

antiyeast drugs are similarly inappropriate. People taking Propulsid
combined with these types of medicines have died from sudden heart
arrhythmias, albeit rarely. Zantac is also very rarely associated with fatal
arrhythmias (and fatal liver damage). Propulsid is dangerous in another
situation as well: it should not be used if there are mechanical obstructions
or perforations in the gastrointestinal tract. In the meantime, I would only
use these excellent medications if the symptoms from the reflux are
themselves significant.

Decreasing the volume and increasing the frequency of feedings is
sometimes adequate to treat reflux. Keeping the baby upright after feedings
is also helpful. Other positioning maneuvers are helpful for some babies.
Thickening the feedings with one tablespoon of rice cereal per ounce of
feeding is an option to discuss with your physician: this can mechanically
reduce the amount of milk sloshed back up the esophagus. Occasionally a
hypoallergenic infant formula gives relief—if a food allergy is involved.
Baby Mylanta, an antacid, is a gentle, pharmaceutical approach to reducing
stomach acid.

RESOURCES

When you need more information on a parenting topic, from
allergies to dealing with divorce to special needs children,
please refer to the following list of organizations. There's a world of
information and help available through these groups. In addition, you'll
find Web sites of particular interest to parents recommended by the
American Medical Association, the U.S. Department of Health and
Human Services, and the American Academy of Pediatrics.

ASTHMA AND ALLERGIES—
Asthma and Allergy Foundation of America

Who: The Asthma and Allergy Foundation of America is dedicated to controlling and finding a cure for asthma and allergic diseases.

What: The foundation serves the estimated 50 million Americans with asthma and allergies through support of research, patient and public education programs, governmental advocacy, and a network of local chapters. It also offers a 24-hour toll-free number for patient information, a bimonthly patient newsletter called *Advance*, patient conferences, school and community training programs, books, and videos. It maintains a large clearinghouse of current and affordable educational materials, such as "Sniffles & Sneezes: A Parent's Guide to Managing Kids' Allergies." Peer support is available in more than 100 local support groups and through the network of affiliated chapters.

How: A one-year membership is $25. For further information, contact:
Asthma and Allergy Foundation of America
1125 Fifteenth Street, NW, Suite 502
Washington, DC 20005
(800) 7-ASTHMA or (202) 466-7643

BREASTFEEDING—*La Leche League*

Who: La Leche League International (LLLI) was founded in 1956 to provide information and support to mothers who want to

ONLINE RESOURCES

ADVICE

http://www.parentsoup.
com or AOL Keyword:
Parent Soup

Parent Soup has lots of
experts and experienced
columnists to answer
any questions you might
have. The site also has a
very active chat and
bulletin board scene, so
you can talk to other
parents (the real
experts) and find out
how they have handled
situations you find
yourself in. You can
come chat with Dr.
Greene, La Leche
League, and a host of
other experts.

breastfeed their babies. Today, the League works with an advisory council of more than 40 health professionals, has consultative status with the United Nations Children's Fund, and advises the World Health Organization.

What: La Leche's mission is to help mothers learn the art of breastfeeding by providing education, encouragement, and mother-to-mother support. Members hope to promote a better understanding of the importance of nursing in the healthy development of the mother-baby bond.

La Leche publishes a comprehensive catalog for new and experienced mothers that offers books, pamphlets, accessories, gift packs, and videos on everything from birth to adolescence. Being a new mother can be a stressful experience, so La Leche is there to lend an ear and provide sound advice on breastfeeding.

How: For a free catalog and information on support groups near you, contact:
La Leche League International
P.O. Box 4079
Schaumburg, IL 60168-4079
(800) LA-LECHE (Monday–Friday, 9 A.M.–3 P.M. CST)
Web site: http://www.lalecheleague.org (See next page.)

CHILD ABUSE—National Committee to Prevent Child Abuse

Who: The National Committee to Prevent Child Abuse (NCPCA) is a nonprofit, volunteer-based organization committed to preventing child abuse in all its forms through providing education, research, public awareness, and advocacy.

What: At the national level, the NCPCA's work includes

- media campaigns,

- research and compiling educational materials, and

- professional training.

At the local level, the NCPCA provides

- direct educational services for parents, teachers, and community leaders about the warning signs of abuse;

- joint efforts with local media representatives to attract attention to child abuse in the state; and

- advocacy for children and families over legal issues and state legislation.

NCPCA offers publications and videos on preventing child abuse. It is also affiliated with support groups and trained specialists who can help prevent and treat abuse.

How: For information about a variety of topics relating to parenting and child abuse, call (800) 394-3366. For

BREASTFEEDING
http://www.lalecheleague.
org

If you're interested in breastfeeding, La Leche League's site is the place to go. It has a terrific FAQ (Frequently Asked Questions) area that will tell you everything you need to know about getting started, plus it provides lots of links. You can ask questions of other moms in chats or on bulletin boards.

r resources

CHILD CARE
http://nccic.org

The National Child Care
Information Center
doesn't have the
greatest-looking site in
the world, but it's a great
place to find the best
care for your kids. It's
also got a research area
that has all the latest
findings on child care.

information on Parents Anonymous, a self-help program for
parents under stress, call (800) 421-0353. For further
information, contact:
National Committee to Prevent Child Abuse
332 South Michigan Avenue
Chicago, IL 60604
(312) 663-3520

CHILD CARE—*Dependent Care Connection®, Inc.*

Who: The Dependent Care Connection, Inc., (DCC®) is dedicated to helping parents find the best possible care for their children's needs.

What: DCC, through its Life Care℠ program, provides experienced
counselors to help parents manage their personal and
professional responsibilities. Staff also work with employers and
human resources, developing key benefits to offer employees and
their families and addressing the changing needs of employee
populations (both in the United States and abroad).

How: For more information, please contact:
Dependent Care Connection, Inc.
P.O. Box 2783
Westport, CT 06880
(203) 226-2680
Fax: (203) 226-2852
E-mail: dccwebmaster@dcclifecare.com
Web site: http://www.dcclifecare.com

CHILD CARE—National Association for Family Child Care

Who: The National Association for Family Child Care (NAFCC) was established in 1971 to apply rigorous standards to child-care centers and programs.

What: NAFCC accreditation requires that day-care centers and after-school programs meet its high standards of child care in these seven areas:

- Indoor safety

- Health

- Nutrition

- Interacting

- Indoor play environment

- Outdoor play areas

- Professional responsibility

Parents can use this organization to help narrow down the field of the best care providers. If you run a day-care program and wish to become accredited, NAFCC will give your organization more legitimacy among parents seeking child care.

DEVELOPMENT
http://lamyourchild.org/
start.html

This resource supplies an interesting look at how kids and their brains develop month by month. You can see where your child stands and what's going to come next. There's also an area for parents to ask questions of experts.

179

r resources

EMERGENCIES AND
FIRST AID
http://www.ama-assn.
org/insight/h_focus/
nemours

The American Medical
Association here
provides a great
reference source for
things like Poison
Control Centers in your
area and emergency
numbers to keep by the
phone. The trick, of
course, is to look at this
site *before* there's a
problem.

How: The cost of applying for accreditation is $225. A one-year
membership costs $20 and includes all publications, insurance,
membership for parents, and extensive networking with providers
and other associations. Contact:
National Association for Family Child Care
206 6th Avenue, Suite 900
Des Moines, IA 50309
(800) 359-3817

DEVELOPMENT—*Zero to Three*

Who: Zero to Three, the National Center for Clinical
Infant Programs, focuses its energies and research
funds on the first three years of a child's life. Staff
members believe that those years are the greatest
time of human growth and development and also the optimal time
for adults to positively influence a child's future.

What: Since 1977 Zero to Three has been internationally renowned for
its work in the fields of medicine, mental health, research, and
child development. Today, the organization supports both parents
and professionals by

- increasing awareness of the importance of these first three
years;

- inspiring tomorrow's leaders and fostering professional
excellence;

- promoting the discovery of new advances in childhood development;

- educating parents about ways in which they can affect their young children's lives;

- assisting Head Start programs serving high-risk pregnant women;

- transmitting new clinical approaches and training to ten thousand worldwide subscribers of the bimonthly bulletin, *Zero to Three*; and

- launching HeartSmart Community Awareness Campaigns, which alert parents, professionals, and policy makers to the importance of early social and emotional development.

How: To receive further information, contact:
Zero to Three
734 15th Street NW, Suite 1000
Washington, DC 20005
(202) 638-1144
Web site: http://www.zerotothree.org

DIVORCED PARENTS—*Children's Rights Council*

Who: The motto of the Children's Rights Council (CRC) is best described by Abraham Lincoln's words: "A man never stands so tall as when

FAMILY RELATIONSHIPS
http://www.parentsplace.com

Lots of experts, articles, and community advice on how to keep you and your family happy and healthy can be found here. Of particular interest is their certified family therapist, who answers questions on keeping your family functioning as a unit.

r resources

FATHERS

http://www.fathersforum.
com

Fathersforum
remembers that there
are usually *two* parents
involved in raising a kid,
and it addresses the
problems that dads worry
about, which many other
sites sometimes ignore.

he leans over to help a child." Founded in 1985, the CRC is dedicated to the rights of children who are members of divorced families.

What: The CRC is concerned with the healthy development of the millions of children of divorced and separated parents. For the child's benefit, the CRC seeks to strengthen families if a separation or divorce occurs. The organization's members work for custody reform by minimizing hostilities between parents and by providing equitable child support. Through advocacy and education they encourage parents to support a child's access to both parents, as well as to the extended family.

Some of the CRC's past achievements include

- testifying before Congress and being credited as the moving force behind the first federal authorization for programs to encourage access (visitation) enforcement;

- developing a resource catalog of more than 75 books, written reports, audio and video cassettes, legal briefs, and children's materials, available to parents at little cost; and

- holding national conferences of prominent professionals from across the country, including researchers, writers, custody-reform advocates, and legislators.

How: A one-year membership is $35 and includes the newsletters *Speak Out For Children* and *Action Alerts*, as well as discounts on materials and conferences. The new member packet contains "The Best Parent Is Both Parents" bumper sticker, a copy of

written presentations from CRC's Seventh National Conference, and a 16-page catalog with discounts on books and reports. Please contact the CRC at:
Children's Rights Council
300 I Street NE, Suite 401
Washington, DC 20002-4362
(202) 547-6227

FATHERS—National Fatherhood Initiative

Who: The National Fatherhood Initiative strives to make responsible fatherhood a national priority.

What: The Initiative publishes *Fatherhood Today*, a quarterly newsletter, updating members on trends in family issues, political and legislative developments affecting fatherhood, and the work of the Initiative. Their information kit provides information that members can use to inform local media representatives about the importance of fatherhood. The community-impact brochure highlights several things that individuals can do to increase the importance of fatherhood in the community. The group also organizes special events and meetings, including a recent "National Fatherhood Tour." By speaking with local leaders and encouraging them to meet with the chairman of the Initiative, Don Eberly, the Initiative has made great inroads in the fight against absentee fathers.

How: To become a member, send a $35 check to:
National Fatherhood Initiative

HEALTH
http://npin.org/respar/
    texts/health.html

This site is all about keeping track of your kid's health. It's got everything from what to expect at a checkup to printable forms that help you keep a day-to-day log of your child's health. You'd have to be a little obsessive to use everything on this site, but that just means that there's something for everybody.

r resources

NUTRITION

http://vm.cfsan.fda.gov/
~dms/wh-infnt.html

It's from the government,
so it must be true.
Everything you need to
know about infant
nutrition and food safety
is right here, plus some
good tips on mom's
health as well.

1 Bank Street, Suite 160
Gaithersburg, MD 20878
(301) 948-0599
Fax: (301) 948-4325
E-mail: NFI1995@aol.com
Web site: http://www.register.com/father or
http://www.fatherhood.org

HEALTH CARE—*Maternity Center Association*

Who: The Maternity Center Association (MCA) is a national, nonprofit
health agency dedicated to the improvement of maternity and
infant care.

What: MCA has been working for more than 77 years to secure high-
quality care for every family and baby before, during, and after
birth.
 Some of MCA's primary goals are

- supporting and conducting research to improve the quality of
maternity services;

- informing and educating the public and government leaders,
thereby providing a balanced view of the needs of American
families; and

- offering classes that prepare expectant and new parents, as
well as siblings, for childbirth and baby care.

MCA's services also provide prenatal, labor, birth, and postnatal care; health education; and nutrition counseling. In addition, MCA's Well Woman Services include gynecological care—Pap smears, pelvic exams, and breast exams.

How: For more information about MCA, please contact:
Maternity Center Association
48 East 92nd Street
New York, NY 10128
(212) 777-5000 or (212) 777-9320

INJURIES—The Injury Prevention Program (TIPP)

Who: TIPP is an educational program designed for parents to help prevent common injuries among children, newborn through age 12.

What: TIPP urges pediatricians to counsel parents about common childhood injuries. The program offers Safety Surveys to help parents identify at-risk situations in their homes. (For instance, parents of newborns are given the "Car Seat Shopping Guide" and the "Infant Furniture: TIPP.")

How: Ask your doctor about the program or, for more information, contact:
American Academy of Pediatrics
P.O. Box 927
Elk Grove Village, IL 60009-0927
(847) 228-5005

PRODUCT RECALL INFORMATION
http://www.notice.com/recalls.html

Even if the crib hasn't been creaking, this site is worth a regular visit. It's a listing of all products that have been recalled recently, and they have an entire area devoted to children's products.

r resources

SAFETY

http://www.aap.org/
    family/tippmain.htm

This site offers monthly
tips on how to keep your
kids safe. It's got
everything from
preventing crime to
making sure a seatbelt
fits correctly. Check out
the rest of the site for
other good articles on
child safety.

INSURANCE—*Insurance Information Institute*

Who: The mission of the Insurance Information Institute is to improve the public's understanding of insurance—what it does and how it works. Funded by insurance providers in the United States, the Insurance Information Institute is a valuable source of information for parents who need many types of insurance.

What: The Institute runs a consumer hotline to answer questions about auto, homeowner, health, and life insurance. It also publishes several informative pamphlets, such as "How to Get Your Money's Worth in Home and Auto Insurance" and "Twelve Ways to Lower Your Homeowner's Insurance Cost."

How: For more information, including a catalog of publications and videos, contact:
Insurance Information Institute
110 William Street
New York, NY 10038
(212) 669-9200 or (800) 942-4242
Web site: http://www.iii.org

MENTAL HEALTH—*Infant-Parent Institute*

Who: The Infant-Parent Institute specializes in the assessment and treatment of problems of attachment in infancy.

What: The Institute, a center for clinical practice, research, and training, also sponsors Mr. Trout's Brief Summer Course in Infant Mental

Health. The research division of the Institute includes the nonprofit Child and Family Research Center, where professionals from clinical, developmental, and experimental psychology, social work, criminal justice, and related fields turn their attention to significant new issues in children's mental health, women's health, treatment outcome, and program evaluation. Among its training activities the Institute also produces several instructional videos and hosts short-term courses in various cities.

How: For further information, contact:
Michael Trout, Director
Infant-Parent Institute
328 North Neil Street
Champaign, IL 61820
(217) 352-4060

MULTIPLES—National Organization of Mothers of Twins Clubs

Who: The National Organization of Mothers of Twins Clubs, Inc., (NOMOTC) has more than 30 years of experience and is devoted to the parents, grandparents, and foster parents of twins and other multiples.

What: Mothers of Twins Clubs are great places to share information and discuss the physical, emotional, and financial problems that often accompany multiple births. The groups offer

- a three-part Support Services program;

- a pen-pal program for mothers who have children with disabilities or illnesses;

- bereavement support to help parents who have experienced the loss of one or more of the multiple-birth children;

- a single-parent outreach offering solo parents the opportunity to share information with others;

- *Notebook*, a quarterly magazine full of stories of multiple-birth families, scientific research, and referrals to experts in the field; and

- the comprehensive Multiple Birth Data Bank, containing information about thousands of multiple-birth sets.

How: For information on membership in your area or to order NOMOTC publications, contact:
National Organization of Mothers of Twins Clubs, Inc.
P.O. Box 23188
Albuquerque, NM 87192-1188
(505) 275-0955
(800) 243-2276
E-mail: nomotc@aol.com
Web site: http://www.nomotc.org

MULTIPLES—Twin Services

Who: Twin Services is an organization geared to aiding expectant parents of twins and triplets.

What: Twin Services offers a help line, newsletters, and a research library. In addition, there is a fee-per-use consultation service, TWINLINE, and you can schedule your own consultation with one of its fully accredited parenting consultants. Twin Services and the TWINLINE help you prepare for

- the birth of the babies—and the upheaval in your routine;

- breastfeeding—and having many mouths to feed at once;

- helping your older children to adapt to the new family members; and

- the disturbance in quality private time between you and your partner.

(You don't need to be a member to use the Twin Services programs, but there is a fee for the TWINLINE.)

How: For more information, contact:
Twin Services
P.O. Box 10066
Berkeley, CA 94709
TWINLINE: (510) 524-0863 (Monday–Friday, 10 A.M.–4 P.M. PST)

NATURAL PARENTING—Be Healthy

Who: Be Healthy, Inc., run by a couple in Vermont, is dedicated to offering natural products for pregnant women, new parents, and babies by mail order.

What: The catalog offers a range of books, tapes, videos, and other products that take an earthy, practical, and sometimes spiritual approach to their subjects. Here are some examples:

- Music and tapes for "inner bonding" that are designed to enhance the development of the unborn baby and increase the bond between pregnant mother and child and between fathers and unborn children

- Herbal teas and other natural products to ease pregnancy ailments

- Exercise videos and equipment to use during pregnancy and after the birth of your child

- Books with practical tips for new parents

- Breast pumps and breastfeeding information to help new mothers get acquainted with the art of breastfeeding

How: For information or a catalog, contact:
Be Healthy, Inc.
R.R.1, Box 172

Glen View Road
Waitsfield, VT 05673
(800) 433-5523

NATURAL REMEDIES—
Homeopathic Educational Services

Who: Homeopathic Educational Services provides health professionals and the general public with access to a comprehensive assortment of information, education, and products that blend natural medicine and traditional science.

What: Homeopathic Educational Services has a catalog of books, tapes, and other products. Among them are these:

- Books and tapes for people who want an introduction to homeopathy: what it is and how to use it

- Books on infant and child health, including *Your Healthy Child: A Guide to Natural Health Care for Children*. These publications are particularly recommended for parents who are concerned about the potential side effects of conventional drugs and who want to learn more about the alternatives

How: To order a catalog or obtain more information, contact:
Homeopathic Educational Services
2124 Kitteridge Street
Berkeley, CA 94704
(510) 649-0294

PENNY-PINCHERS—Welcome Addition Club

Who: The Welcome Addition Club was established to help new moms with its many resources.

What: The Club provides breastfeeding and formula-feeding moms with extra support—from day one through your baby's first birthday. The Club is free, so joining might be one of the best decisions you make during this important growth period. Some of the benefits of joining are

- Similac with Iron, Infant Formula Starter Supply;

- money-saving coupons for Similac with Iron, Similac Isomil, or Alimentum Protein;

- a toll-free "Babyline" with tips, gifts, and special offers; and

- a free Rosco Teddy Bear.

How: For more information, just dial the "Babyline" at: (800) 222-9546 and ask about the Welcome Addition Club Special Offer.

POSTPARTUM DEPRESSION—Depression After Delivery

Who: Depression After Delivery is a national self-help organization founded to provide information and support for women and families suffering from postpartum distress.

What: Local support groups meet twice a month to share their personal experiences, discuss medical resources, and lend a friendly, supportive ear. The national organization also functions as a clearinghouse of information, supports a national telephone line, and publishes a quarterly newsletter.

How: Membership costs $30. For more information, contact:
Depression After Delivery
P.O. Box 1282
Morrisville, PA 19067
(800) 944-4773 or (212) 295-3994

POSTPARTUM DEPRESSION—
Postpartum Support International

Who: Postpartum Support International (PSI) is an international network that focuses on postpartum mental health and social support.

What: PSI's aim is to provide current information to members on the diagnosis and treatment of postpartum mood and anxiety disorders. PSI also helps advocate research into the etiology, diagnosis, and treatment of postpartum mood and anxiety disorders, as well as provides education about the mental health issues associated with childbirth. The organization encourages the formation of support groups.

　　In addition, PSI offers *Postpartum Mood and Anxiety Disorder: A Research Guide and International Directory*, a publication containing more than 300 pages and 1,300 references about postpartum depression, as well as many other video and book titles.

How: Membership in PSI is $30 (U.S. and Canadian individuals),
$45 (group), and $50 (professional), and the fee pays for
quarterly newsletters and discounts at the annual PSI Conference.
Make checks payable to:
Postpartum Support International
927 North Kellogg Avenue
Santa Barbara, CA 93111
(805) 967-7636

PRODUCT SAFETY—U.S. Consumer Product Safety Commission

Who: The U.S. Consumer Product Safety Commission (CPSC) is an
independent federal regulatory agency founded to protect the
public against unreasonable risks of injuries and deaths
associated with consumer products.

What: The Commission has jurisdiction over 15,000 products, from
automatic-drip coffeemakers to toys to lawn mowers. It works to
reduce the risk of death and injury from consumer products by

- developing voluntary standards with industry groups,

- issuing and enforcing mandatory standards (and banning
products if there is no feasible standard to protect the public),

- obtaining the recall of products or arranging for their repair,

- conducting research on potential hazards, and

- informing and educating consumers.

The Commission operates about 40 regional offices in the United States and runs a toll-free hotline that the public can use to request information on product recalls and what to look for when purchasing a product or to report an unsafe product.

How: To receive a publications list, send a postcard to:
Publications List
CPSC
Washington, DC 20207

To request specific publications or to report a faulty product, call the hotline at:
(800) 638-2772 or send E-mail to Info@cpsc.gov

SINGLE PARENTS—*Parents Without Partners*

Who: Parents Without Partners is a nonprofit organization devoted to the welfare and interests of single parents and their children. There are more than five hundred chapters worldwide, ranging in size from 25 to 3,000 members. Participants are male or female; custodial or noncustodial; separated, divorced, widowed, or never married.

What: Each Parents Without Partners chapter provides group discussions, lectures, and workshops, as well as single-parent family activities such as picnics, hikes, and camping trips. The adult activities allow single parents to meet and exchange parenting stories. Parents Without Partners also publishes *The Single Parent* magazine, holds an annual convention for all chapters, provides $500 scholarships for teenagers of single parents, and acts as an advocate.

How: Contact:

Parents Without Partners International, Inc.

401 North Michigan Avenue

Chicago, IL 60611-4267

(312) 644-6610

E-mail: pwp@sba.com

Web site: http://www.parentswithoutpartners.org

SPECIAL-NEEDS CHILDREN—The ARC

Who: The ARC is the new name of a 44-year-old organization formerly known as the Association for Retarded Citizens of the United States. Formed in 1950 by a small group of parents and other concerned individuals, the organization has always been devoted to improving the lives of the mentally retarded and their immediate families.

What: The ARC is involved in programs for

- enforcing the Americans with Disabilities Act,

- educating prospective parents about preventing retardation (especially from fetal alcohol syndrome), and

• working with educators on teaching strategies for the retarded.

How: A one-year membership is $15. To begin receiving brochures and additional information, make your check payable to:
The ARC
National Headquarters
500 East Border, Suite 300
Arlington, TX 76010
(817) 261-6003

SPECIAL-NEEDS CHILDREN—*Parents Helping Parents*

Who: Parents Helping Parents (PHP) is an organization devoted to parents who have children with special needs due to illnesses, accidents, birth defects, allergies, learning problems, family problems, or family stress. PHP is a United Way Agency and a Presidential Point of Light organization.

What: Through PHP membership, you will receive these benefits:

• Valuable information on your child's specific disability

• Referrals on how to get the best care for your child or teenager

• Training vital for communicating with health-care professionals

• A place to talk with other parents, just like you, who have "been there," understand your feelings, and can take time to listen

- Financial-relief information to help cope with added medical expenses

- Advocacy skills to protect the rights of your child

- Assistance in starting or developing other family resource centers

PHP can make a difference if you are coping with such afflictions as attention deficit disorder, fetal alcohol syndrome, Down's syndrome, hearing or respiratory problems, and seizures. PHP provides access to online computer services, national resource directories, and a guide to special-needs libraries. Most important, PHP assures you that you are not alone in raising your special child.

How: An annual membership is $35 ($60 for professionals). For further information, contact:
Parents Helping Parents
The Family Resource Center
3041 Olcott Street
Santa Clara, CA 95054-3222
(408) 727-5775

STAY-AT-HOME MOMS—
Formerly Employed Mothers at the Leading Edge (FEMALE)

Who: FEMALE is a support group dedicated to mothers who are leaving the full-time workforce in order to channel their intellect, time, and energy into the career of motherhood.

What: FEMALE has more than 145 chapters nationwide, providing women with a place to share friendship, concerns, and a sense of community. Chapters offer

- regular meetings with topical discussion groups, guest speakers, and book discussions;

- play groups;

- family outings;

- Mom's Night Out activities;

- baby-sitting co-ops;

- a membership directory;

- support systems in times of personal need; and

- volunteer management opportunities.

FEMALE also hosts message boards and chats at Parent Soup as a network for mothers to meet one another and talk about their lives as well as to satisfy the urge to talk to someone over three feet tall.

How: To find a chapter near you, or to start one of your own, contact:
FEMALE (Formerly Employed Mothers at the Leading Edge)
P.O. Box 31
Elmhurst, IL 60126
(630) 941-3553
E-mail: femaleofc@aol.com
Web site: http://members.aol.com/femaleofc/home.htm

STAY-AT-HOME MOMS—MOMS Club

Who: MOMS Club is a national, nonprofit support group for stay-at-home
mothers of all ages who are interested in learning a variety of
activities for themselves and their children—and who are proud of
their decision to stay at home. The MOMS Club has more than
14,000 members in 300 local chapters across the country, and
more chapters are registering every week.

What: MOMS Club is a unique women's organization: it is the only
national support group for all at-home mothers. The chapters
meet during the day when mothers at home need the most
support and interaction (mothers should feel free to bring along
their children!). Local chapters have business meetings, park
days, baby-sitting co-ops, play groups, and other activities
(depending on what the members want for their local club).

How: To find a club near you or to start your own club, please enclose
$2 to cover costs and write to:
MOMS Club

25371 Rye Canyon Road
Valencia, CA 91355

STAY-AT-HOME MOMS—Mothers at Home

Who: Mothers at Home was founded in 1984 by a group of young
mothers who recognized that some of the most intelligent and
motivated women they knew were making the decision to devote
their time to raising their children yet were feeling isolated and
misunderstood.

What: Mothers at Home maintains a strong and effective voice both in
public policy discussions and among media representatives by

- challenging the "typical housewife" and "typical working
  mother" stereotypes, as well as the misuse of statistics
  regarding the care of children;

- researching the needs and attitudes of at-home mothers
  through detailed surveys that are forwarded to policy makers
  and media; and

- influencing national legislation by consulting with congressional
  aides and testifying before congressional committees.

Mothers at Home publishes a members' newsletter, *Welcome
Home*, as well as two books, *What's a Smart Woman Like You
Doing at Home?* and *Discovering Motherhood.*

How: For more information, membership, and subscriptions, contact:
Mothers at Home
8310A Old Courthouse Road
Vienna, VA 22182
(800) 783-4666
E-mail: MAH@netrail.net
Web site: http://www.netrail.net:80/~mah/

SUDDEN INFANT DEATH SYNDROME (SIDS)—
Sudden Infant Death Syndrome Alliance

Who: The Sudden Infant Death Syndrome Alliance is a national, nonprofit health organization dedicated to the support of SIDS families, education, and research.

What: Parents can obtain a free brochure on how to reduce the risk for SIDS. The Alliance has a nationwide, 24-hour, toll-free information and referral hotline. There are also local affiliates that provide support services.

How: To reach the hotline, call (800) 221-SIDS (7437). For further information, contact:
SIDS Alliance
1314 Bedford Avenue, Suite 210
Baltimore, MD 21208
E-mail: sidshq@charm.net

WORKING MOTHERS—9 to 5

Who: 9 to 5, a membership organization for working women, combines grassroots activism with cutting-edge research and sophisticated media work to win real changes in the workplace.

What: The organization 9 to 5

- provides a toll-free hotline for job problems with free counseling on legal rights for working women;

- pioneers educational projects to improve job efficiency, performance, and satisfaction;

- publishes numerous books and reports on issues ranging from contingent work to sexual harassment; and

- puts out the *9 to 5 Newsletter*, which contains job advice, charts trends in office work, and provides other useful information.

(The film *9 to 5*, starring Dolly Parton, Lily Tomlin, and Jane Fonda, was based on stories told to 9 to 5 problem counselors.)

How: Annual dues are $25. For more information, contact:
9 to 5 National Association of Working Women
238 West Wisconsin Avenue, Suite 700
Milwaukee, WI 53203-2308
(414) 274-0925
(800) 522-0925

SCHEDULES *(See also Sleeping)*

New parents dream of having their baby on a schedule that calls for two two-hour naps a day and a good eight hours of sleep every night. Unfortunately, babies have their own agenda, and you can't type up a memo, take a vote, or even beg them to change it. All you can do is try different approaches, such as to how often you feed them, what you feed them, or how long you let them nap, until you find a routine that works for you. More likely, this means until your baby starts going longer between feedings and sleeping longer at night through the miraculous growth process.

Problem: Asleep During the Day, Awake at Night

Q: We just became new parents 10 days ago, and ever since my daughter came home from the hospital, she seems to have her days and nights mixed up. She sleeps the whole day but at night she only sleeps about two hours at a time. Any suggestions to get her (and us!) sleeping through the night would be greatly appreciated.

~ *Parent Soup member Flyboy6657*

Alter the Environment

A: You need to reprogram her. Keep your house bright and noisy during the day, then quiet and dark at night. Also try to keep her up a little more during the day. Hope this helps!

~ *Brandi G., Lake Worth, Florida*

DR. GREENE'S INSIGHT: Brandi's suggestion makes a big difference. You might also try touching her feet often during the day (whether she's awake or asleep) and avoiding this during the night. Also, make eye contact with her frequently during the day (she will find this very stimulating—better than coffee!). Then at night, feed and cuddle, but avoid eye contact.

Try a Little Cereal?

At seven weeks, our son was getting up only once a night (I know, we were lucky!) and sucking tremendous amounts of formula, five to eight ounces per bottle. I started mixing one teaspoon of rice cereal per ounce, with a maximum of six teaspoons. Not only did he tolerate it well, he *loved* it and immediately began sleeping through the night. Try a cereal bottle at bedtime and see if that helps.

~ *Renee C., Fayetteville, Arkansas*

I tried giving my son rice cereal at seven weeks also because I was desperate for some sleep, but it didn't work. He had no kind of schedule at all until five and a half months, when he just started sleeping through the night and taking two two-hour naps during the day. In those first few weeks you're pretty much just a slave to their schedules.

~ *Parent Soup member RhettsMom*

Keep Baby Up During the Day

When we brought our son home from the hospital, he had the same problem. Well, I guess we had the problem, since my husband and I weren't getting much sleep. I was breastfeeding the baby, so I called our local breastfeeding hotline. They suggested making sure that he nurses every three hours during the day—which meant waking him up from naps during the day. I tried it, and it worked immediately! I don't know if you are breastfeeding, but even if you aren't, try waking her up from

> **DR. GREENE'S INSIGHT:** The Academy of Pediatrics recommends that you do not add rice cereal to the bottle for most babies. Among other things, it fools a baby's mechanism for knowing how many calories to take in. Kids who have had cereal in the bottle struggle with weight issues later in life more than kids who don't get cereal in the bottle. You get a short-term advantage by doing this but a potential long-term disadvantage.

naps during the day to make sure she is eating enough and not sleeping too much during the day.

~ *Teresa C., Pittsburgh, Pennsylvania*

Sample Schedule

At three months old, my son's feeding schedule looked like this: eight-ounce bottles at 7:30 A.M., 11:30 A.M., 3:30 P.M., and 7:30 P.M. He slept from 8:30 P.M. until 7:30 A.M.

~ *Lisa K., Tucker, Georgia*

Cutting Out Nighttime Feedings

My friend's baby got in the habit of having a bottle in the middle of the night, due to illness. When the baby was well and my friend knew her baby didn't need the late night bottle anymore, she just cut back an ounce a night. Within a week, no more nighttime bottle. She has done this with both her kids, and it worked both times—one child stopped waking up, while the other cried for a short time before going back to sleep.

~ *Cindy J., Eugene, Oregon*

I made the mistake of nursing my first child to sleep. Notice that I said *mistake*. It got to the point that as he got older, he would sleep only if I nursed him. Then it went to rocking and holding, then (after moving from his crib to a bed) I would have to lie down with him. By reading quite a few parenting books I have since learned that most parents use the following routine: nurse or feed—nap—playtime.

But my experience has taught me that it should instead go like this: nurse or feed—playtime—nap.

I used this method with babies two and three. When they were eating every three hours, I would feed them, make them stay awake for playtime for about an hour or so, then put them down for a nap. They would then sleep until their next feeding. And now I have no problems putting either of them down for naps. It is so nice when they can put themselves to sleep without needing a bottle to do it!

~ *Patricia M., Anchorage, Alaska*

Conditioning Baby to Sleep

Sssh, baby's asleep! Not necessarily. Although you might think it's necessary to tiptoe around the house while your baby's napping, it's not necessary. If your baby gets used to sleeping in a perfectly quiet house, he'll come to expect it.

~ *Ann Marie M., Lincoln University, Pennsylvania*

SEPARATION ANXIETY

Every baby goes through clingy phases, when you can't put your baby down without her freaking out. Surely you're tired of hearing "It's just a phase," but that's exactly what this is. One solution is to put your baby in a sling or other carrier and just carry her until she starts to relax a bit without your holding her. Just as for colic, in many cases contact equals comfort. Of course, if you're working (or in any other number of scenarios), this method isn't for you. Instead you've got to soothe your baby as much as you can and grin and bear it until "this too shall pass." Just remember, before you even know it, that same baby will be running out the door, tossing a casual "Bye Mom" over her shoulder, and you will be left wondering how she could have ever been too attached to you.

The Problem

Q: My son is seven months old. Anytime I leave the room and he can't see me, he starts having a mental breakdown. I absolutely go crazy because I cannot get anything done. Is this just a phase?

> ~ *Parent Soup member TLHugs*

A Solution: Teaching Baby to Play Independently

A: My daughter is nine months old, and she can play by herself for about 20 minutes. Then she can come check on me, and when she sees that Mommy is "alright" she usually goes back about her business. Of course, she was not always this way, and there are times when she needs to be held. You have to teach your baby to play independently. Try putting her with a couple of toys in a high chair next to you in the kitchen while you're cooking. Another thing you can try is putting her in a playpen (if you've got one) for 5, then 10, then 15 minutes; she will learn to entertain herself.

> ~ *Natalia W., Metairie, Louisiana*

Waking Up Screaming

Q: My 10-month-old son has started waking up from his second nap of the day screaming bloody murder. When I pick him up, he immediately puts his head down on my shoulder and wants to go back to sleep. I hold him on my chest for a few minutes and he falls asleep. When I go to put him back in his crib, he sits up and starts to cry. If I keep him on my chest, he will sleep for quite a long time. What should I do? I know babies want to be held, but I also want to be careful not to establish poor sleeping habits. Any advice?

> ~ *Teresa C., Pittsburgh, Pennsylvania*

Keep Them Close for a Little While

A: That is the age when my children entered their severe attachment
phase. I never really found anything to help soothe them, other than
letting them sleep on my chest. It only lasted a month or so. I figure,
this is the only time in their lives that they'll actually want to cuddle.

   ~ Parent Soup member The Mommi

Keeping Your Sanity When You're Always in Demand

Q: I am a working mother of a nine-month-old. I went back to work after
my daughter was four months old. In the past couple of months my
daughter has become extremely "clingy." She exhibits this behavior
only toward me. As soon as she sees me, she wants me to carry her. At
times she has cried for up to 10 minutes if I'm busy fixing dinner or
doing other chores. My husband is a great father. He's the one who
takes her to day care (since I leave very early in the morning). When
I'm not around, she's happy playing on the floor with him or just
being silly. As soon as she hears my voice or catches a glimpse of me,
this normally happy baby turns into a cranky one, crying nonstop
until I pick her up. This behavior is causing me a great deal of
frustration. I'm also tired from constantly attending to her when I'm
around her. Please help before I go crazy.

   ~ Liz R., Fremont, California

DR. GREENE'S INSIGHT

A: **Calling yourself a working mother is an understatement! All mothers work,
but when you work outside the home as well, you are holding down two
different kinds of jobs. For many mothers, their work outside the home is
refreshing and gives them energy for their demanding job at home. Some**

mothers long to be home with their children and only work outside the home because they feel they must. Whatever your situation is, it is normal for you to feel extremely tired, especially when your little one wants you whenever you are near.

Now, the good news. What your daughter is going through is a common, limited phase of child development. Many children strongly prefer one parent over every other person in the world for a brief period of time. Usually they prefer their mothers for a period (ranging from approximately one month to several months) during the later part of their first year. During this particular time, your daughter's desire for you is especially intense, as she is in the midst of a developmental phase characterized by separation anxiety. After children grow out of this stage, many of them will prefer their fathers over everyone else on the face of the earth. Usually the period of attaching to their fathers is shorter than the period when only their mothers can make the world a better place.

During this very taxing time, you may want to consider ways that your family can adjust its lifestyle to help you (and your daughter) through this:

- Don't try to get too much done during the periods you are alone with your daughter. Use this time to build an even stronger relationship between the two of you.

- Adjust the family dinnertime so that you don't start cooking until after Dad has come home and had a chance to unwind.

- Have Dad or another responsible adult take your daughter out of the house for an hour or so each day so that you can have a little time to do the things you need and want to do (like prepare dinner), without her crying to be picked up.

- Decline invitations to events that don't fit your family's current needs. If you really must or want to go to the event, consider hiring a baby-sitter for the evening. As long as you are spending focused time with your daughter each day, it's OK to get a sitter occasionally in the evening, even if your daughter is in child care during the day.

- It's OK to let her cry some. Trust your maternal instincts. If you would rather adjust what you are doing and pick her up, do so. At those other moments when your deep desire is to get something accomplished, do what it takes to proceed. If you listen to your deepest desires and act accordingly, she will learn both that you love her intensely and that other people, too, have needs.

- When she starts to cry, breathe deeply, remind yourself that this is only a phase, and think about the parts of being a mother that you enjoy the most!

One day, in what I am afraid is the very near future, you'll remember the time when you were the center of her world and all the tiredness and frustration you now feel will seem a small price to have paid.

SEX *(See also Fertility After Giving Birth)*

OK, let's cut right to the chase. *Yes*, it is possible to be a parent and have a healthy sex life. And a good sex life at that, even a great sex life. But there's no $19.95 miracle pill that will bring back your libido and get you and your partner back on track. The number of parents who talk about their impaired sex drive on Parent Soup's message boards attests to that. So don't think you're the only one wondering if you'll ever again have sex with your partner. Take heart: for every message of despair, there's a message of hope from someone who's reckoned with her new body and new role and come out the other side with a sexual intimacy that's better than ever. You may even want to jump ahead and read Parent Soup member Mary Eileen M.'s post in the sidebar. That woman knows what being a parent and a sexual being is all about! And as you read through the rest of the stories and suggestions here, get ready to do a dance of joy. You are already on your way to that great-sex sex life you were dreaming about.

Lack of Libido

I think part of the problem is fatigue, and some of the fatigue is mental, not just physical. For women, sexuality starts with the need to be touched, and if you have kids you are getting touched plenty. You simply don't have that physical hunger that you used to have for someone to touch you. I know that by the end of the day, I don't want any more human interaction. I have been touched and interacted with to death!

~ *Isadora, Maryland*

From reading so many posts I am amazed at all of us women who have had children and now have no sex drive! We are all so frustrated because no one can seem to help us. I thought it was just me, and it makes me feel better that this isn't only my problem. Tons of women are going through the same thing (and husbands, too).

~ *Darla L., Grafton, Ohio*

I can relate. Our daughter just turned 12 weeks old, and I am nursing her. I have very little desire (if any) for a sexual relationship. Here's why: (1) I AM TIRED! (2) I am so totally repulsed by my own body that I cannot imagine someone else getting pleasure from it. (3) Because I am nursing, I think my husband is terrified to touch my breasts, as if they are *off limits* or something. The baby consumes our life and that's the way it is for now. Hopefully, someday we will be able to resume our sex life.

~ *Shaun B., Greenville, South Carolina*

Prescriptions for Romance

Your husband won't go near your breasts? He must be crazy! When my wife was breastfeeding, I found them incredibly attractive!

~ *Jeff L., Raleigh, North Carolina*

Suggestion: Invite your husband to do all he wants with your breastfeeding breasts—touch, caress, suck, and so on. Mine was intimidated until I let him know that I thought it was great! That was seven years ago, and now we both really miss nursing!

~ *Carol S., Woodinville, Washington*

Tell your husband all the wonderful things he does for you. Name at least five things—men don't get enough good comments from us now that we are so busy. Name five parts of his body that you like. Tell him, and watch his face light up. It worked for me!

~ *Connie G., Lilburn, Georgia*

After I had our first child, my husband spent a lot of time at the office, saying that he needed to work overtime. But what I found out was that he didn't know how to react with the baby because he had always had all of my attention, and now all I had energy for was the baby. Don't worry. It will get better; husbands just need time to adjust.

~ *Alane J., Brooklyn, New York*

Two in the shower can do wonders! Enjoy!

~ *Parent Soup member ASTOR651*

We have two kids—both under the age of two and a half. I know what it feels like to be extremely tired and not in the mood for sex. My husband and I have found that you just have to grab a little hug here, a kiss there. It's not the most exciting sex life, but we make sure to show each other that we're still attracted to each other and there for each other.

~ *Page S., Houston, Texas*

Sex after having children can and will be fantastic, as long as you make an effort. After the doctor has declared you fit to resume intercourse, experiment with your new body. Often foreplay will feel different. You and your husband may need to get to know your body all over again. And how often do you get to do that with your own husband? Go slowly and ask for patience from your partner. Make a date for the two of you to have some fun, preferably at a time when you are not overly tired.

~ *Marie T., Asheboro, North Carolina*

Changing Bodies, Changing Sensations

Q: This is kind of embarrassing, but I hope someone can help. Since I've had children, sex just isn't the same. I feel a little stretched out inside and I also get very wet. Any suggestions?

~ *Amber H., Savannah, Georgia*

A: One of the best things you can do is Kegel exercises. That's where you tighten your vaginal muscles and hold for 10 seconds. You do sets of 10 during the day. It is something you can do no matter where you are. It helped me.

~ *Lisa M., Hixson, Tennessee*

A: Yes, you get stretched out! Imagine having a baby's head come through there and not stretching? The amazing thing is that with proper exercises, you can get tighter again. You need to strengthen your vaginal muscles. Next time you are urinating, stop it midstream: it's that muscle. Exercise it at stop signs, while online, in line at the grocery store, washing dishes, wherever.

~ *Jackie B., San Jose, California*

Beyond the Physical

Sex is so much more than just being in the mood and doing it. It starts way before then with communication: not simply surface talk, but about how you feel and what drives and motivates you. For a woman, sometimes honest, open communication with no ulterior motives can be more of a turn-on than anything else. You start to bond more with your spouse and fall more deeply in love. And when you can't describe in words anymore how much you love him, then sex communicates it for you.

~ *Val W., Mercer Island, Washington*

After 16 years with my wife, I know that there are periods when spouses are simply not in sync with each other. These periods will last from a week to a month or more. Usually, when you get alone and real quiet so you can think, you begin to realize what's bothering you, such as the kids have been especially hard to manage or the job particularly stressful or

POWER OF
THE DARK

Being a mother of four and
sporting the telltale signs of
three C-sections, I would just
like to praise the advantages
of the dark. I am 38 years
old, and though I have
finally managed to lose the
weight that being pregnant
and eating M&M's can add
over the years, I still face the
aftereffects of the migration
of my flesh and the sad fact
that stretch marks truly do
look better stretched.

So when faced with the
advantage of knowing in
advance that I will be in
sexual contact with my
darling husband, you can bet
that the lights go out (with
the exception of one very
important candle)! It is not
so much that I delude myself
in believing that this dear
man, who has seen me in the
buff for the last 20 years,
does not know the hills,
valleys, dimples, and dents

whatever. But these phases will happen and will pass if you stay your
course and fall back on the one true friend you have—your spouse.
You just can't let sex rule the marriage. One good thing about all
this, though, is that getting back in sync is really fun!

~ *Bill, Minnesota*

As your marriage matures, you need to come up with new ideas of
what you think is romantic. Yeah, love notes, flowers, and special
surprises are great. But let's face it—how realistic are they? Jobs,
households, and kids tend to put the typical ideals of romance low on
the totem pole. Find a new list of things that make you feel romantic
and are a turn-on. For instance, occasionally my husband brings me
a cup of coffee before I get out of bed. Sometimes he is standing in
the bathroom holding my towel and robe for me as I get out of the
shower so I don't get cold. It means he was thinking of me and took
the time to do something to show me. I love seeing the look on his
face as he interacts with the children. It's so tender and gentle, it
makes my heart do flip-flops. What's more romantic than making
and bringing children into the world together? There is a lot of
romance in the little things, if you just start looking for it.

~ *Lisa K., Tucker, Georgia*

My definition of romance is not to think so much in terms of sex as
romantic feelings. My husband and I have totally different schedules,
but I can usually find a few moments to grab him and give him a kiss,
even while passing through the garage on my way out the back door!
I have even approached him while he is mowing the lawn, acting like
I need to talk to him a moment, only to sneak in a kiss on his sweaty
face!

Try not to think so much of what you are not getting, but instead of what you can give! The simple things, like a hug, a kiss, an I-love-you, are the things that start the romance back in your life. Don't dwell on the lack of sex; that's not romance!

~ *Cheri, Washington*

Possible to Have a Sex Life in the Family Bed?

Q: My baby is sleeping in the same room with us. My fiancé thinks it's OK to have sex while the baby is in the room, but I am not so sure. Anyone else in this situation, or does anyone have any advice?

~ *Jennifer, Texas*

A: Relax about having the baby in the room! Trust me, the dear little one will never know what is going on, and hopefully it will reinforce your relationship with your partner, which only makes things better for the baby!

~ *Patti F., Enterprise, Alabama*

SLEEPING

I think lack of sleep is the hardest, most horrible side effect of being a new mother—who knows how different it would be if we had our sleep!

~ *Mary L., Dorchester, Massachusetts*

Honk if you agree with this statement! Sleeping is one of the great paradoxes of parenting—you pray for the day when baby will sleep

of this aging body, but that in the dark, well, I transform amazingly. I am not what the light reflects back to me from the full-length mirror of my closet door, but something altogether different.

The light of one candle, strategically placed (no less than 17 feet from the bed) illuminates the illusion of my younger self. I am capable of movement equal to gold-winning gymnasts, with an allure surpassed by few. Yes, in the dark, I am Woman, hear me roar!

Now, I am not saying that I will pass up the opportunity to connect with that sweet man if the light is still shining and the blinds are not drawn, but give me the light of one candle, a locked door, a little bit of time, and the only dimples this man is going to remember are the ones on both our smiling faces!

~ *Mary Eileen M.,*
West Long Branch,
New Jersey

through the night. You develop a whole repertoire of sleep-inducing rituals: you hum, you rock, you long to sleep until 7 A.M. And then the day comes when you aren't awakened in the middle of the night. Do you rejoice? Well, yes, but not until after you've woken with a start, convinced that something terrible has happened to your baby in the middle of the night. This is yet another area where babies simply won't be rushed to accommodate our schedules. In the meantime, here are the top 10 ways that Parent Soupers send their babies off to sleep.

Top 10 Sleep Inducers

1. Let Them Sleep Where They Want to Sleep

My daughter hated her crib in the beginning. So I started putting her in her baby carrier at night. She slept all night long there. It looked uncomfortable, but it worked. I kept her in her carrier right next to my bed for the first few weeks, then moved it into her room so she'd get used to sleeping there. At about eight weeks, I moved her into her crib with no problem.

~ *Ragene M., Easley, South Carolina*

2. Swing to Sleep

My two kids would sleep only in their swings when they were babies. I figured I should let them sleep where they were comfortable. With my first, I didn't start putting her in her crib until 9 or 10 months, and boy, what a screamer! With my second, she lived in the swing until she was four or five months old, and then we started putting her in her bed even though she fussed. It only lasted a little while, and to this day (now 18 months) we can just pop her in her bed and she goes to sleep without a problem.

~ *Angela K., South Bound Brook, New Jersey*

3. How to Put Them Down Without Waking Them Up

I was just giving my husband some hints yesterday on how to put the baby down without waking her up. Here's what I found to work with both our girls:

● Swaddle her in a thin, fuzzy flannel blanket. Then, when you put her down, there is no change in temperature.

● Whichever way she is resting on me when she falls asleep, either belly on my shoulder, on her back, on her side, is how I put her in the cradle. That way the pressure she has fallen asleep with is still there when I put her down.

● If she starts to stretch while I am waiting for her to hit deep sleep, I take advantage of her moving and inch my way closer to the cradle or change hand positions if it will make it easier to put her down.

  ~ *Susan B., Ridgefield, Connecticut*

If you nurse, cuddle, or rock your baby to sleep, the temperature change between your warm body and the cold sheets may be enough to wake her. We warm up a receiving blanket in the dryer for a few minutes and then put it in the crib, so that when we put our daughter down, she stays nice and warm (and rarely wakes up once she's in the crib).

  ~ *Susan H., Syracuse, New York*

4. Let Them Realize Where They Are Before You Leave the Room

One of my twins was falling asleep in our arms and waking up in his bed, and it basically freaked him out. Our pediatrician suggested that we lay him down while he was half asleep, let him realize where he was, and comfort him if he needed it but not take him out, and gradually he would fall asleep on his own. And that after a while we would be able to put him down awake and he would put himself to sleep. Yeah, right, easier said than done! It was hard at first, but we kept it up and, yes, it actually works now. But it sure doesn't work overnight.

    ~ Megan, Minnesota

5. Set Up a Comforting Sleep Environment
We have a crib light that we turn on when our 11-week-old is fussy—it works wonders. She stares at the light for a few minutes before drifting off. I have a heating pad in her crib that I put on low for a few minutes *before* I put her in the crib. That way, her crib is nice and warm, and there's no wake-up shock from cold sheets.

    ~ Joanne P., St. Petersburg, Florida

6. Try a Fish Tank
Get your child a small fish tank with a light. At night set it up where he can watch the fish swim. It not only acts as a night-light, but it also gives him something to look at while he falls asleep.

    ~ Cheryl C., Glenwood Springs, Colorado

7. Calming the Anxious, Tired Baby
Our three-month-old screams bloody murder whenever he is tired. The only thing that works for us is to first make sure that he is in fact tired, not in pain or in a wet diaper. Then either my husband or I will lie down and hold him stomach-down on our chest and hum in a very steady, low tone. He screams for a bit, but he gradually begins to listen to the vibrations coming from our chest and his crying subsides

until it disappears. We hold him very securely to the chest or it
doesn't work. It takes about three minutes for him to settle down,
but it works!

> ~ *Lisa B., Bensalem, Pennsylvania*

8. Swaddling Clothes
Swaddling works well with my twins when they can't sleep. They are five
weeks old now, and they love being wrapped tightly. I think it is the
security; I was told that babies can get frantic in the beginning when their
arms and legs are flailing all over the place.

> ~ *Megan, Minnesota*

9. Minimize Waking in the Family Bed
Our daughter sleeps with us, and we've learned that she doesn't wake up
as much if she sleeps next to Dad instead of me.

> ~ *Debbie W., Albuquerque, New Mexico*

10. Teaching Baby How to Put Himself to Sleep
Many times a baby grows used to waking up during the night to eat. A
baby after the age of four months can safely sleep through the night
without eating, as long as you feed baby as close to midnight as possible.
Sleeping through the night means five to six hours. Keep that in mind.
Also, as difficult as it seems, I believe in the 20-minute quick-check
method. That is, when the baby first cries, you let her cry for one or two
minutes. (I actually had to use a stopwatch. It felt like forever.) Then go
in, check diaper, burp, and if all is OK, put her back in crib and leave
the room. When baby cries again, wait two to three minutes, go in, but do
not pick the baby up. Pat her on the back, make sure she's OK, then

leave. Baby cries again, then wait five minutes, then do the same thing. You continue this "heartbreaking" process for up to 15 to 20 minutes. If baby still hasn't stopped, go in and quiet her until she sleeps. The next night do the same procedure, but start off waiting five to six minutes. Next night, wait seven to ten minutes before going in. It usually lasts no more than a week. The baby will begin to realize that it is bedtime. I know it sounds cruel, but babies know they are adorable. They get into habits, just like adults. We need to teach them how to put themselves to sleep, just as we teach them everything else. Hope this helps, and of course, it's just my opinion.

~ *Patricia M., Anchorage, Alaska*

Now that you've learned some ways to get back to sleep, here are some ideas for dealing with the shock you'll inevitably feel the first time your baby (and therefore, you) sleeps through the night.

When It Finally Happens

When my son first slept through the night, I woke up panicking like a nut because he hadn't awakened yet. I ran into his room, did the whole check-to-see-if-he's-breathing routine, and when I couldn't even tell because he was sleeping so soundly, I picked up his little hand to see if it was cold (I know it sounds morbid, but I think every mother out there knows what I am talking about). When he finally started moving his lips a little bit, I was so relieved! After that night, he slept every night the whole way through!

~ *Parent Soup member LoriDeCa*

When your baby won't fall asleep in her own crib, you usually . . .

Of 961 total votes

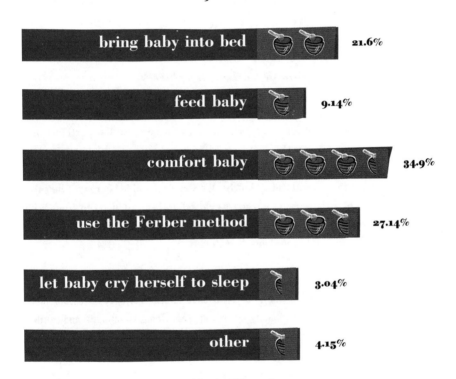

bring baby into bed	21.6%
feed baby	9.14%
comfort baby	34.9%
use the Ferber method	27.14%
let baby cry herself to sleep	3.04%
other	4.15%

1 bowl = 100 parents

PARENT SOUPERS' MOST CREATIVE LULLABIES

Rock a bye Connor
 On Mommy's lap.
 You're really fussy,
 It's time for a nap!
Mommy will rock you
 Til you pass out.
 Then you won't need
 To wiggle and shout.
 ~ *Jennifer H.,*
  Orchard Park,
  New York

Rock-a-bye Katie.
 It's time for sleep.
 Just close your eyes
 And start counting
  sheep.
Mommy is tired and
 Daddy is too.
 We'll get to sleep
 Just as soon as you
  do.
 ~ *Janemarple*

The worst is when your baby decides to sleep through the night, and you're so exhausted, you do, too. And when you wake up in the morning and realize the baby hasn't been up all night, you hop out of bed and run to her room, and she is sleeping as happy as a clam while your heart is beating a mile a minute!

~ *Linda S., Mesa, Arizona*

Rice Cereal in the Bottle to Help Baby Sleep?
[See also Schedules]

Q: My daughter is six weeks old and cries all the time, particularly at night. My sister says that I should put rice cereal in her bottle before bedtime, and that this will make her sleep better. My pediatrician says it's best not to start solid food for some time and advises against putting rice cereal in her bottle. My sister says this is crazy. She says that this is the way my niece was raised and she turned out fine. What do you recommend?

~ *Laurie P., Hoboken, New Jersey*

DR. GREENE'S INSIGHT

A: Other parents have a wealth of experience to offer us. They have seen many things that worked and many that didn't. Their input is valuable and worth considering carefully. Still, since the time they were raising their children, many new facts have come to light. Listening carefully to the wisdom and insights of other parents and weighing them against the latest findings of science will often lead you to the best course of action.

During the previous generation or two, when bottle-feeding became very popular, solid foods were introduced at quite an early age. When babies were as young as a few weeks old, processed rice cereal was put into the bottle with formula. Most children were able to tolerate this rather well. But some did not, because their sucking and swallowing actions were not yet fully coordinated. As a result, many infants aspirated the rice cereal into their lungs, which led to pulmonary problems.

Now, based on the wisdom of experience and the latest scientific knowledge, the Academy of Pediatrics recommends that solid foods be introduced in general no earlier than four months of age. If a child weighs at least 13 pounds and has good head control, solid foods can be started as early as three months. Four months old isn't the magical date to start solid foods: it is fine to start later than that or, in some cases, as early as three months. At about this age the caloric needs of a baby increase up to 24 to 32 ounces of breast milk (which is impossible to measure, but babies do an excellent job getting just the right amount) or formula, plus as much solid food as she wants. The best way to tell the right timing to start solid food is when your baby seems to be asking for it. She is not likely to say, "Mom, can I please have solid foods?" It is more likely that when you are eating she will look at you as if to say, "How come you aren't giving me some of what you are having?" This communication will likely be in the form of fussiness when you are eating. This is a good time to begin solid foods.

The Academy of Pediatrics does not recommend putting rice cereal in a bottle, but instead feeding it to a baby from a spoon. Rice cereal can be purchased in jars, as a dry mix, or you can prepare your own by cooking rice without salt or seasoning and pureeing it in a food processor or blender. If you choose the dry mix, the rice-cereal box will have directions for mixing it in the correct proportions with either breast milk or formula for baby's first meal—which is very diluted. As the child gets older, the cereal can be mixed into a thicker consistency.

With the rice cereal mixed, place your daughter in a propped-up position and move the spoon toward her mouth. The first few days she will tend to push the cereal right back out with her tongue. This is because

This may not be a lullaby, but my mom made it up and we have sung it for years. Using the tune of "When the Saints Go Marching In," just sing "La la la la light, la la la la light. . . ." You get the idea. My daughter loves to dance to it and now knows what and where a light is. She points at the light to get me to sing it!

~ Danielle S.,
Negaunee,
Michigan

babies have a thrust reflex, causing the tongue to thrust back out anything that is put in their mouths. Take plenty of videos of this very cute stage because it passes quickly. Within several days your daughter will begin to get the idea of closing her lips around the spoon and swallowing. Once she does, you can begin to monitor the amount of food she needs. In order to determine this (which is not a predetermined amount but one that varies from child to child), keep moving the spoon toward her mouth and look for signs that she is losing interest. If she turns her head away, clamps her lips shut, or appears bored, it is time to stop. Otherwise, keep moving the spoon to her mouth as long as she keeps opening it and looking happy.

It is interesting to note that children who begin solid foods with rice cereal in their bottles don't learn the instinct of stopping when they are full. This is because deceptively large amounts of calories come in without much increase in volume. As a result, kids that are fed rice cereal in a bottle tend to have excessive weight gain, both as infants and later in life. Other than that, children are very good at regulating their own intake. By starting with a spoon, resting between bites, and stopping when your child is full, you will be laying an excellent foundation for good eating habits throughout her life.

SOLIDS

Dr. Greene and the American Academy of Pediatrics suggest that it's best to wait to introduce solid food until after a baby is four months old (see the previous question on rice cereal under Sleeping). If you try to feed your baby solids before then, you will probably notice the reason why experts recommend waiting until four months—babies have a tongue-thrust reflex that causes them to push right back out anything that goes in their mouth (other than a nipple). While this display may make for a good home video, it doesn't make for a good meal.

The book *Feed Me, I'm Yours* was mentioned numerous times on the message boards as a great resource for recipes, feeding strategies, and more. It's by Vicki Lansky, and it gets a five-Soup-bowl approval rating (the highest score) from Parent Soup!

How to Know They're Ready for Solids

The basic rule of thumb I follow as to when to start solids is to wait until they try to grab stuff off my plate.

~ *Chelsea S., Spring Hill, Tennessee*

Starting Out

Cheerios are a perfect first finger food. They dissolve quickly and also help hand-eye coordination.

~ *Kristi M., Dallas, Texas*

Introduce one food at a time, so that you can discover any sensitivity to certain foods.

~ *Kristy S., Portland, Oregon*

Sneaking Fruits and Vegetables into Your Child's Diet

Both of my sons, now two and three, have been devoted to this following recipe since their first birthdays, and must have it every morning. They drink three cups of it each! Heaven help me if I'm out of bananas.

1 ripe banana

8 to 12 oz. milk

Put in the blender and blend until very smooth. Vary amounts and add tofu or whatever pleases you. It's a cinch if you keep the blender handy.

~ *Pamela H., Pacific Palisades, California*

I've found a great way to give my son all kinds of fruits and veggies in finger-food form. Take any cooked veggie or fruit and mash it up. Add to pancake batter and cook it like a regular pancake. You can then either tear the pancake into bite-sized pieces or use as a whole. I did this with bananas this morning, and he tore through them like a hurricane. He ate four pancakes, a record!

~ *Angela S., Shreveport, Louisiana*

Making Your Own Baby Food
I have two kids, ages four and one. I have never owned a food processor, and I found it easy to make baby food myself. The first foods I fed my daughter were bananas, carrots, and squash. I mashed a well-ripened banana with a fork, then added a little bit of water, and mixed it until smooth. For carrots and squash, I sliced and steamed them in a frying pan with a little bit of water, then covered it. It doesn't take long, even if you don't have fancy kitchen gadgets! You can mash ripe peaches the same way as bananas, and when the baby's old enough, you can add green veggies. I almost always steam vegetables; boiling takes away the nutrients. Canned fruits and vegetables have almost *no* vitamins and are loaded with sugar and salt. You'll be surprised by how much money you save.

When my daughter was about nine months old, I began chopping and mashing spaghetti with meat in it, macaroni and cheese, or chicken and rice. Just avoid heavy spices and salt. For dessert or snacks, I give my kids applesauce (no sugar added), or I fix instant pudding. I am just as busy as the next person, but it's important to take the few extra minutes to prepare healthy meals.

~ *Melanie, Virginia*

I have twins and literally could not afford to feed them jars of baby food! It was costing me $12 a day (my little piggies)! So I put meat (steak, chicken, lamb, or pork) and vegetables in a big pot with water and let them cook for one to two hours. The meats really need to cook a long time. I put the cooked meat in the blender and then in ice cube trays, then in Ziploc bags, dated. You can really make some interesting combinations.

~ *Christine O., White Plains, New York*

Scrambled egg whites, soft peas, cut-up carrots, and rice are favorites of my daughter (eight months). Bits of pasta with the sauce on the side for dipping also works well. She just got to the point where she wants to feed herself, so I make her cereal or instant potatoes and let her feed herself. Who cares about the mess? Small pieces of skinless chicken breast are good too. Just put out small amonts at a time and add to it as it is eaten; otherwise it may be shoved in the mouth all at once!

~ *Andrea B., Ft. Lauderdale, Florida*

A Feeding Schedule with Formula and Solids
My son is seven months old and has been on solids since he was four months. Presently, his schedule looks like this:
7:30 A.M. One serving of cereal with half a banana mashed; 6 oz. bottle

**SUGAR-FREE
RECIPE FOR
GRAHAM
CRACKERS**

2¼ cup whole-wheat
    flour
¾ cup whole-wheat
    pastry flour
1 teaspoon baking
    powder
½ cup butter
⅓ cup honey
⅛ cup molasses,
    unsulfured
1 teaspoon vanilla
1 teaspoon cinnamon
½ cup mik

In a bowl, combine the
two flours and add
baking powder. In
another bowl, cream
together the butter,
honey, molasses, vanilla,
and cinnamon. Cream
until fluffy. Add flour
mixture and milk

11:30 A.M. Half jar of veggies (or veggie and meat) and
       half jar of fruit; 4 oz. bottle
3:30 P.M. Same as breakfast (sometimes yogurt, tofu); 4 oz. bottle
7:30 P.M. Bedtime bottle (8 oz.)

My first step was to drop his late bottle (10:30 P.M.) and make it four bottles a day of 8 oz. each. I started cereal only at 11:30 A.M., then I added veggies and fruit at 3:30 P.M., then added the cereal at breakfast last. I always feed him his solids first, then his bottle. As he became more interested in solids, he started to take less formula. I kept making the large bottles for a while, but the above quantities were all he would consume. Hope this helps.

~ Cristin Z., Oceanside, California

DR. GREENE'S INSIGHT

After your baby has done well with cereal for a week or two [see the question in the Sleeping section for information on introducing cereal], other solids can be introduced, as long as he is at least four months old. Strained vegetables are the next foods to be introduced—mostly peas, green beans, squash, sweet potatoes, potatoes, and carrots. Give your baby only one new food at a time. Be sure to wait three to five days before starting another one to determine if he has any reaction to a food, such as a rash, stomach pain, vomiting, or diarrhea. If you are going to prepare vegetables at home for your baby, you should not prepare carrots, beets, turnips, or collard greens. In many places these vegetables contain large amounts of nitrates, which can cause anemia in infants. (The vegetables used in prepared baby foods do not contain these nitrates.)

Your baby may not take to these new taste sensations immediately. If you drink coffee, you probably remember the first time you took a taste—it was horrible! Many baby foods that we consider bland have the same impact on children's extremely sensitive taste buds. When it comes to introducing new foods, breastfed babies have an advantage, since the taste of Mom's milk varies depending on what she has eaten. Formula-fed babies get the exact same taste every time they drink a bottle, and the introduction of new foods can be particularly difficult for them.

The best way to get your infant to eat a new food is to desensitize him to the taste. You can accomplish this by using the new food for his first bite of solids each day for 10 days straight. The first day he might take one mouthful and spit it out. The second day, he will usually swallow the first mouthful but might refuse more of that food. The third and fourth days he will probably take a few bites, but will undoubtedly want a food to which he is already accustomed. If you continue this pattern for 10 consecutive days, most children will acquire a taste for the new food—even vegetables!

Tip: While your child is in the process of learning to eat a new food, try scooping a small portion of it into a bowl and serving your child from the bowl. If you dip a "used" spoon into food, you can't store it for later use because it may be contaminated by bacteria. Never force a child to eat more of a new food than he is ready for, but always be ready to scoop up more if he is still interested!

Children between four and six months of age should be fed solid foods once or twice a day. The ideal timing for one of the feedings is 30 to 60 minutes before bedtime. This will produce the maximum drowsiness for an excellent night's sleep. After solids have been introduced, baby should continue to take 24 to 32 ounces of breast milk or formula every 24 hours. It is not a good idea to add sugar or salt to his food or bottle (unless treating a specific problem). Most bottle-fed, five-month-old babies will take five- to six-ounce bottles, four to six times per day. They can often go eight hours at a stretch once during a 24-hour period.

alternately to the creamed mixture. Mix well after each addition. Chill for several hours. Divide dough in half. Rechill one portion while rolling out the other half. Roll on a lightly floured board to $\frac{1}{8}$-inch thickness. If dough becomes too soft while working with it, rechill it. Using a knife or a pastry wheel, cut dough into three-inch squares. Prick each square three times with a fork. Do this on the other half of the dough. Bake at 325 degrees Fahrenheit for about 30 minutes. Cool and store in an airtight container. Makes 40 crackers.

~ *Judie, New York*

S solids

TRIVIA QUESTION

Unlike adults, babies
don't have to worry
about this:

a. Peanut butter

b. Cholesterol intake

c. Sugar intake

d. Sodium intake

e. Food allergies

Answer: b

*Cholesterol is essential to the
development of the nervous
system, but cut back on it as
baby grows.*

Warning! Two Foods That Babies Should Not Eat
DR. GREENE'S INSIGHT
Stay Away from Honey

Honey should never be given to infants less than 12 months old. The concern is infant botulism. Botulinum spores are widely found in soil, dust, and honey. Adults who swallow botulinum spores are almost never affected. When infants swallow the spores, however, the spores can germinate in their immature gastrointestinal tracts and begin producing botulinum toxin. This has occurred even when the honey was only used to sweeten a pacifier.

Infant botulism has been found on every continent except Africa. In the United States it is most common in the states of California, Utah, and Pennsylvania. While infant botulism can occur from taking in soil or dust (especially vacuum-cleaner-bag dust), eating honey is the number-one preventable cause.

Infant botulism can occur any time in the first year of life, but it is most common in the first six months. In fact, it has been suggested as the cause of death in up to 10 percent of SIDS cases (Nelson, *Textbook of Pediatrics*; Saunders 1992).

The first symptom of infant botulism is constipation (which is also a common benign finding in many infants). This can appear three to thirty days following ingesting honey containing the spore (*The AAP Red Book*, 1997). Typically, the parents then observe increasing listlessness, decreased appetite, and weakened crying over the next several days. Nursing mothers often report new engorgement. Sometimes this is the full extent of the disease. If the disease progresses, however, the child moves less and less and might begin to drool from the mouth. Gagging and sucking reflexes diminish. Loss of previous head control is also an important sign. Complete respiratory arrest can occur either suddenly or gradually. If an otherwise healthy baby develops constipation, followed by weakness and difficulty in sucking, crying, or breathing, then infant botulism should be considered the most likely diagnosis until proved otherwise.

Thankfully, if the botulism is correctly diagnosed and the baby receives appropriate supportive care, almost all infants will recover fully and completely.

Be Careful with Strawberries

I want to post this in case there are other first-time moms who may also not know what I didn't know—although I seem to be the only person who was unaware of it! Do not feed babies who are less than a year old strawberries. My doctor told me I could start ice cream and yogurt, so I gave her a tiny bit of strawberry ice cream, thinking she eats raspberries and blueberries, so why not strawberries? The ambulance was at my house in 10 minutes. (Strawberries are apparently a highly allergenic food.) The nurses at the emergency room looked at me like I was crazy for feeding her that. And I feel like I flunked Motherhood 101 big time. Anyway, maybe this will prevent someone else from going through what we went through.

~ *Amy W., Greenwich, Connecticut*

> **DR. GREENE'S INSIGHT:** While some babies do have serious allergic reactions to strawberries, you shouldn't feel bad if you've fed your baby strawberries. Doctors aren't yet in agreement as to the best age to introduce them. Many feel that nine months is fine. The other highly allergenic foods to be careful about are nuts, peanut butter, shellfish (which should not be given before the first birthday), and, in some cases, eggs.

SPITTING UP *(See Reflux)*

SPOILING *(See also Crying and Colic)*

A common fear among parents is that they will spoil their baby if they come running every time the baby cries. The thing about babies is that they are completely helpless without their parents and hence need to be, well, babied. Babies are little bundles of needs, and while there are limits to how much one parent can do for a child, fulfilling these needs will ensure baby's healthy growth and development.

DR. GREENE'S INSIGHT

Very young children cannot be spoiled. Some babies have greater needs than others due to their physical conditions, but all babies are very needy! Crying is their only way of communicating these needs with us. If babies didn't cry when they were hungry or needed their diaper to be changed, we wouldn't know of their need.

As babies grow, they begin to communicate things other than physical needs. This includes the desire to be held or comforted and the desire to be stimulated. When babies express a need, you will not spoil them by taking care of the need. In fact, it is important to meet their needs to build their sense of security, love, and trust. You also will not spoil them by giving them what they desire—unless you always give in to them, even when you don't want to. Now this is the hard part: It is good to give a baby what she wants sometimes, *but not all the time*. So how do you know when to respond and when not to? A general rule of thumb is to ask yourself if you are *giving* your baby what she wants or if you are *giving in* to what she wants. In most cases, if you are giving just because you want to give, you will be doing the best thing for your baby.

Watch for being so stressed by your other children, job, or whatever that you never feel like giving to your baby. At the other extreme, watch for finding your identity so much in your baby that you always feel like giving *in* to her.

Rethink Your Definition of "Spoiled"

Try not to think of a baby who wants to be held a lot as being "spoiled." The most natural place for a young baby to be is in close physical contact with other people, mainly mom.

~ *Yolanda D., Wausau, Wisconsin*

STRANGER ANXIETY
(See also Separation Anxiety)

All of a sudden, it seems, your outgoing baby turns incredibly shy. He will freak out if anyone is holding him other than you or your partner. It goes hand in hand with separation anxiety: suddenly baby realizes who takes care of him, and being away from that person (even in the hands of someone who's sitting right next to that person) is terrifying to him. It can start as early as six months but generally hits between eight and ten months.

Time Heals All Anxieties

My son used to cry when he saw anyone but his mom and dad. It got to the point where we couldn't even have any of the grandparents baby-sit for us. I am sure that you don't want to hear, "It will go away in time," but I don't have any better advice to give. It lasted about a month with my son. As long as we held him, he would stop crying.

~ Melissa S., St. Charles, Missouri

Don't Force the Issue

My daughter just got over this stage. If she started to cry when grandparents or friends came over, I would hug or touch them and tell her, "See, they are OK." It took a couple of days with her first grandpa, but it was OK because I let her go at her own pace. *Major advice*—do not insist that strangers or grandparents hold your child if that stresses your child. This will delay the transition.

~ Parent Soup member Tis me1972

235

SUDDEN INFANT DEATH SYNDROME

When Parent Soup polled parents about what they worried about the most during those first few months, the overwhelming response was that the baby would stop breathing (nearly 71 percent). Technically known as sudden infant death syndrome (SIDS), this cessation of breathing in babies is hard to predict (hence the *sudden*) and therefore becomes an easy target for parents' anxieties. Dr. Greene addresses these fears and explains the probable causes of SIDS and the best ways to prevent it.

DR. GREENE'S INSIGHT

Becoming a parent opens up new landscapes within us: new hopes, fears, delights, and sorrows. Suddenly we realize how fragile life is, and worry settles in and becomes part of our lives as we realize that sometimes, even if we do everything right, babies die. There is no magic moment when you will stop worrying. But these feelings also make us realize how precious each life is.

SIDS, or sudden infant death syndrome, is defined as the sudden, unexpected, and unexplained death of any infant or young child. It is the most common cause of infant death in developed countries, accounting for about half of the deaths that occur between one month and one year of age. The current SIDS rate is 1.3 per 1,000 live births in the United States.

Possible Causes

Many factors can combine to cause SIDS, but most of the infants have a damaged or immature brain stem, making it difficult for them to wake up when they are in trouble. Even before the baby is born, anything that causes less oxygen to get to the baby in the uterus will increase his or her risk. On average, smoking during pregnancy doubles the chances, and the odds increase with each cigarette.

Other drugs of abuse, such as cocaine or heroin, increase the risk by as many as 30 times.

After birth, a baby's susceptibility to SIDS is influenced by many things. SIDS is more common in babies who are bottle-fed, who sleep in warm environments, who are overbundled, who sleep in rooms with space heaters, who are exposed to cigarette smoke, who sleep on soft surfaces, who do not use pacifiers, and who sleep facedown or in a prone position. The rate of SIDS is also higher in those babies who do not receive timely well-child care and immunizations.

PARENT POLL

When you were a new parent, what did you worry about most?

Of **878** total votes

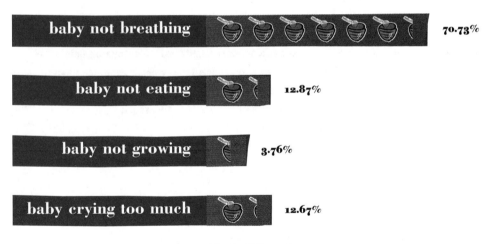

baby not breathing — 70.73%

baby not eating — 12.87%

baby not growing — 3.76%

baby crying too much — 12.67%

1 bowl = 100 parents

There are other contributing factors outside of our control. Genetics plays a large role. The syndrome is more common in boys than in girls, and it is more common in some population groups (Black, Native American, Hawaiian, Filipino, Maori).

Preventive Measures

Putting children to sleep on their sides or backs lowers the risk of SIDS by about three times. Use firm bedding in a slightly cool room. Avoid cigarette smoke and even anything that smells like cigarette smoke. Take your baby in for regular, well-child visits and immunizations.

Those parents who do smoke can give an invaluable gift to their children by stopping. I understand that tobacco can be a real addiction and that stopping can be a monumental task. But minimizing our children's exposure to smoke is well worth the effort and expense.

There is no way to completely prevent or even predict SIDS. This uncertainty makes the deep love we have for our children all the more poignant. The peak period for SIDS is between two and four months old. It is very rare before one month of age, and at least 95 percent of all cases occur before children reach six months old. But this doesn't mean that when they pass six months, all fear will subside—life will always be both strong and fragile, a treasure to be cherished moment by moment.

SURVIVAL TIPS

In all those daydreams you had about having a family during all those nine months when you looked forward to your impending arrival, you probably imagined swaddling a cozy, cooing baby who looked up at you with adoring eyes and slept for at least six hours at a stretch. You probably didn't imagine having an emergency C-section, being unable to get baby to eat, enduring projectile spit ups, having no time to bathe, or any of the other millions of ways your parenthood would not go according to plan. Raising a baby may just be the toughest job you've ever had, made even tougher by the idea you once had that it would be so blissful. So here's the section you read to get a little perspective from parents who have learned that, like life, having a baby is never quite what you expect yet is more than you could have hoped for.

Reality Check

When I learned I was pregnant, I started looking forward to a vaginal birth and breastfeeding my baby. Well, to make a long story short, I ended up not only having an emergency C-section but also being unable to breastfeed my son. I was a wreck. When I told my OB how disappointed I was about not having endured natural childbirth, she looked at me and said, "Would you like me to break your arm? Do you think enduring pain will make you a better parent?" I always look back on that and laugh. But finally, I did learn to get my priorities straight. Having a child is not about surviving natural childbirth or rigidly adhering to the latest child expert's parenting advice. It's about having a healthy little person to share your life with.

~ Barbara V., Boulder, Colorado

No Time for a Shower?

Q: When do *mothers* of new babies bathe? Seriously, I have a friend who has a newborn, and she never has any time to herself!

~ Christine D., Philadelphia, Pennsylvania

DR. GREENE'S INSIGHT

A: The addition of a new baby throws the family rhythm into a tailspin! Moms, dads, and siblings often feel their needs aren't being met as the new baby requires much of everyone's time and attention. Remember that every member of the family has valid needs, not only the new baby. Dad may need to have an extra half hour to unwind after work before diving into family time, since family time now requires so much energy. An older sibling may need daily, one-on-one time from each parent to feel secure. Mom and Dad may each need some time set aside daily for their grooming routines to maintain positive self-images. It is a good idea for the family to talk about the changes the new baby has brought and tell each other about their new needs. Then they can discuss how to work together so everyone's needs can be met. Having said all that, here are a few suggestions regarding time for the mother of a newborn to bathe:

- Many children are comforted by the sound of running water and will sit peacefully close by while Mom or Dad takes a shower. Make sure the baby is dry, fed, and comfortable. Then put the baby in an infant seat or car seat. Take the little bundle into the bathroom, so the baby can see Mom or Dad and hear a parent's voice. When the baby gets a little older, games of peekaboo work very well from the shower!

- Set aside a time each day that is Dad's special time to spend with the baby and Mom's time to take care of her own personal needs. Establish a period that is long enough for Mom to really feel that she has had a

240

break, but not so long that Dad feels abandoned. Even a brief amount of time can make a huge difference to a new mom! (Hint: consider including a five-minute soak in a steamy, mineral salts bath. It can seem like an hour to tired muscles.)

- Arrange to trade child care with another new mom from your neighborhood on a regular basis. If both babies spend an hour with one mom, then an hour with the other, each mom has one very busy hour and one hour to herself. It is ideal if both moms live in the same building or on the same block, but be creative.

- If you don't know of other new moms in your area, you may find older neighbors who are unable to spend time with grandchildren of their own and would love to spend time with your baby on a regular basis. Including them in your extended family can be a wonderful, mutually beneficial relationship.

- Find out if Dad's company offers paternity leave so the two of you can share more of the responsibility for the baby in those precious first few weeks.

What works for one family may not work for the next, particularly if it is not a traditional family configuration. Experiment and observe until your family comes up with solutions that work for you!

No time to shower? Purchase a see-through shower curtain. You can watch your baby through the curtain while you bathe.
    ~ *Ann Marie M., Lincoln University, Pennsylvania*

Keeping Perspective
Here's a poem for everyone to ponder:
> Cleaning and dusting can wait for tomorrow,
> Cause children grow up, we've learned to our sorrow.
> So settle down cobwebs, dust go to sleep;
> I'm rocking my baby, and babies don't keep.

> ~ *Sheila K., Florissant, Missouri*

Taking Time to Relax
All parents, but especially stay-at-home parents, need some time off. When you think about it, a stay-at-home parent is on call 24/7. When you and your children have some time apart, you can all reenter the fray with new energy. So don't feel guilty! Take a walk, read, work on a craft, treat yourself to lunch out, call a friend, or whatever. Once my son was old enough, I took him to a day-care center for three afternoons a week. We could barely afford it at the time, but I needed it. I found my patience level increased dramatically. He also had the chance to interact with other children. I felt guilty at first, but as time went on, it did us both a lot of good.

> ~ *Marc N., Staten Island, New York*

And You Thought You Couldn't See Because You Were So Tired?
Just a note to new moms—after all three kids were born, my eyesight seemed really awful. I went to the doctor, got glasses, and it was great— for about eight months. Then my eyes weren't as good as I thought they should be. But my insurance only covers glasses every two years, so I just ended up wearing the old ones. Finally, a different eye doctor told me that pregnancy can change your eyesight temporarily, but it will usually go back to normal. Wish I had known that before!

> ~ *Ellie M., Wendell, North Carolina*

TEETHING

Just when you start getting into a routine, the teeth start coming in. The baby starts sleeping less (as if that were possible). He starts gnawing on anything that stands still. And he is obviously in some pain. Below are some surefire ways to ease the discomfort, as well as some guidelines from Dr. Greene as to when you should start seeing those teeth come through. (For information on what to do after the teeth come in, please turn to Tooth Care.)

How to Tell It's Starting and Ease the Pain

When my son first started teething (at about four months), he was extremely fussy and got a rash on his chin from drooling so much. He also stopped sleeping all night and was putting everything in sight in his mouth. Here are some things that worked for us:

1. Gently massaging his gums with my finger. For the first couple of minutes he didn't like it, but then he realized the pressure felt good.

2. A frozen teether (it looks like a double popsicle). We tried the plastic teething rings with gel inside, but immediately nixed them because he poked a hole in it and the gel ran out.

3. Baby Anbesol or Orajel helps in a pinch. Although he hated the taste, it did seem to relieve some of the pain.

4. We froze a wet washcloth and then let him chew on that.

5. When things were really out of hand and he couldn't calm down, we used Tylenol.

6. Sometimes, though, all he wanted was to be held close.
~ *Lisa, Ohio*

My almost-four-month-old girl has been teething for two weeks now. I find that walking her around the house calms her down, as does handing her over to her daddy.
~ *Laurie P., Hoboken, New Jersey*

I use Hyland's teething tablets (homeopathic chamomile pills, available in health-food stores). They work great in those early teething stages. You just put them under baby's tongue and let them dissolve.
~ *Joleen, Washington*

Try putting Orajel on a teething toy. Then when the baby bites it, the medicine will rub off on his gums.
~ *Jennifer V., Methuen, Massachusetts*

I know a surefire way to ease your little one's teething pain. Open your minds because this is going to sound really kooky, but I know from experience that it really works. Put the teething gel in your child's ear. Yes! In your child's ear. If you were to stick your index finger in your ear and just let it reach naturally, the curve that your finger tip will be touching is where you rub the teething gel in. This works because the same nerve endings that are in that spot in your ear are also in your gums. No more struggling with your child, trying to pry the little mouth open. My kids actually come to me and offer me their ears whenever they have teething pain now. It is unbelievable. If you

> **DR. GREENE'S INSIGHT: I** haven't heard this suggestion before, but it just might work! The ears and gums are connected (some people feel gum pain in their ears). If you try this with your kids, please stop in one of my chats at Parent Soup and let me know if this works!

don't believe me, try it on yourself. Then the next time your baby is screaming at three in the morning, try it on her.

~ *Rhonda N., Louisville, Kentucky*

Late Teethers
I have a nine-and-a-half-month-old who finally cut his two bottom teeth at eight and a half months. He had all the symptoms of teething since four months. So don't worry, the teeth will come in!

~ *Rip W., Summit, New Jersey*

I thought my son had gums of steel—he didn't start getting his teeth until after his first birthday. Now my eight-month-old has no teeth and no signs of any coming. And I didn't lose my last baby tooth till I was 15! Maybe the teething process runs in the family?

~ *Melissa S., St. Charles, Missouri*

DR. GREENE'S INSIGHT

Many parents worry about the timing of the appearance of their children's teeth. While on average the first teeth appear between five and seven months of age, there is a wide, normal variation of timing. The teeth might come in as early as one month of age, or they might wait until a child is almost one and a half years old. Anywhere in this range can be normal.

Lower teeth generally come in before upper teeth, and girls' teeth erupt earlier than those of boys (much like with everything else). Delayed eruption of all teeth may be the result of a nutritional problem (such as rickets) or a systemic condition (such as hypopituitarism or hypothyroidism).

Some babies are born with teeth. Known as *natal teeth*, they are found in about one of two thousand newborn infants. These are often extra teeth, but this should be confirmed radiographically before any attempt is made to remove

245

TRIVIA QUESTION

Which is *not* a sign that baby is teething?

a. Excessive drooling

b. Minor coughing

c. Excessive sleeping

d. Ear pulling

e. Low-grade fever

Answer: c

Unfortunately, the sensitive gums can bring back the much-dreaded nighttime waking.

From Parent Soup: The Game

them. Natal teeth may cause pain to the infant, poor feeding, and, if the baby is nursing, maternal discomfort. Natal teeth may also cause damage or even amputation of the tip of the newborn's tongue due to strong sucking behavior. Early appearance of all teeth may indicate a hormonal problem, such as hyperthyroidism.

The following table outlines the normal ranges for teeth to erupt.

ERUPTION OF PRIMARY OR DECIDUOUS TEETH

Upper	6 to 8 months
Lower	5 to 7 months
Central incisors	8 to 11 months
Lateral incisors	7 to 10 months
Cuspids (canines)	16 to 20 months
First molars	10 to 16 months
Second molars	20 to 30 months

THRUSH

Thrush is simply another term for yeast infection. It can be quite painful—breastfeeding mothers who suffer from thrush call the sensation it gives them exquisite pain. Babies can't say what it feels like for them, but the increased fussiness that often accompanies thrush indicates that they don't like it much. Here are ways to identify and treat this persistent infection.

How Can You Tell It's Thrush?

Q: My three-and-a-half-week-old baby girl has a few white spots on the insides of her cheeks and lower lip. Is this thrush? The spots don't seem to bother her. Is there any treatment necessary, or is this a normal condition that will disappear on its own?

~ *John, Yokohama, Japan*

DR. GREENE'S INSIGHT

A: At your daughter's age, thrush is the most common reason for spots in the mouth such as you've described. Thrush is a superficial yeast infection that is found in about 5 percent of healthy newborns. Infants usually acquire the yeast from their mothers during passage through the birth canal. The yeast is more apt to remain in those infants who abrade the lining of the mouth with prolonged sucking (such as babies who sleep with a bottle or pacifier). Visible thrush begins to develop seven to ten days after birth. The use of oral antibiotics, especially during the first year of life, can lead to recurrent or persistent thrush.

The lesions of thrush are white (or sometimes gray) plaques found on the insides of the cheeks, the lips, the tongue, or the palate. If the only symptom is a uniformly white tongue, it isn't thrush. The plaques of thrush are often described as curdlike. Unlike milk residue, they adhere to the underlying tissue.

Thrush lesions can be quite painful, leading to a baby's fussiness and decreased feeding. They can also be completely asymptomatic. Either way, the yeast sometimes passes through the gastrointestinal system and causes a yeast diaper rash on the other end.

In otherwise healthy children, thrush is a self-limited condition, usually resolving within a month from its first appearance. No treatment is required.

Even though it will improve on its own, treatment is often recommended either to alleviate oral discomfort or to treat (or prevent) painful yeast diaper rashes.

Treatment usually consists of an antifungal medicine, such as nystatin suspension. This can be gently applied directly to the plaques, with a cotton-tipped applicator, or given orally (two ml four times daily). Another form of treatment calls for using a cotton-tipped applicator dipped into a mixture of one-fourth teaspoon of baking soda and one or two drops of mild liquid detergent (without ammonia or bleach) mixed in a glass of warm water.

Stronger medicines are available though usually unnecessary. If the thrush persists, yeast on the nipples or pacifier should be considered as possible sources for reinfection. Nystatin can be placed on the mother's breasts; artificial nipples and pacifiers can be sterilized.

Don't Treat Only the Baby

We went though four cases of thrush before I realized that yeast will live on everything! Don't forget to boil (better yet, get new) pacifiers if your baby has any. And make sure *you* are being treated, too (rub nystatin on your nipples after every feeding). Otherwise, you and the baby will just pass the infection back and forth. When we gave our daughter her medication, we used a Q-tip with the medicine on it and rubbed it on the white patches.

~ Ann Marie M., Lincoln University, Pennsylvania

Yet Another Use for Vinegar

When we got thrush, my lactation consultant recommended washing my sheets, my clothing, and everything else that the baby came in contact with, using vinegar in the rinse cycle. And she recommended that we take gauze and water and wipe the thrushy patches off before we applied the medicine.

~ *Tarrant F., Eugene, Oregon*

Modify Your Diet
I have had a lot of experience with recurrent thrush that's breastfeeding-related and non-breastfeeding-related (I take an inhaled steroid for asthma that gives me oral thrush, despite my best efforts). Two things that have helped keep thrush at a manageable level (and even get rid of it) are cutting way back on sugar in the diet (yeast lives on sugar) and taking acidophilus capsules (available at health-food stores). These are in addition to the regular medical routes. It really helps speed the process.

~ *Jacqueline C., Sydney Forks, Nova Scotia*

Wandering Thrush
My daughter had thrush for the first month of her life. Once you start treating the oral thrush with medication, it travels through the baby's digestive system and results in a diaper rash. I recommend you go ahead and get a nystatin prescription for the diaper area as well.

~ *Chantel A., Auburn, Washington*

THUMB SUCKING *(See also Pacifiers)*

Better than many adults, your baby knows how to calm herself down—all she has to do is suck on something. And what better than something that is attached to the end of her arm? She can find her thumb at any time of the day or night, and she doesn't need you to do it. It's a popular point of view to think that a baby who sucks her thumb is needy or weak, but it may be more accurate to say that she is self-sufficient. Dr. Greene explains the baby's need to suck.

How Can I Stop My Child from Sucking His Thumb?

Q: My six-month-old has never taken a pacifier. I breastfed him for four and a half months. Now, he is sucking his thumb. He really sucks it hard when he is sleepy and even sometimes when he is comfortable and content sitting in his chair. How do I break this habit? He cries when I snatch it out of his mouth. Will this pass? Please say there is a cure. I do not want him developing buckteeth from thumb sucking. Help!!!

~ *Maria M., Brooklyn, New York*

DR. GREENE'S INSIGHT

A: When ultrasounds were first performed on pregnant women, one of the first things we saw was that babies suck their tiny thumbs even before they are born. Infants are hardwired to need and enjoy sucking as a separate experience from feeding. This need is more pronounced in some infants than in others. Infants tend to exhibit the sucking behavior most when they are tired, bored, or in need of comfort. Some babies who do not suck their thumbs can be comforted, stimulated, or put to sleep through pacifier use. This is often more acceptable to parents since they can control the use of pacifiers. The problem with pacifiers is that young babies cannot find them when they fall out of their mouths, which happens quite frequently. Babies who use pacifiers are dependent on an adult who must understand their needs and respond to them. *Children who suck their thumbs are able to begin at an early age to meet their own need for sucking. These children fall asleep more readily, are able to put themselves back to sleep at night more easily, and sleep through the night much earlier than infants who do not suck their thumbs.*

Many parents worry that their children won't stop thumb sucking at the appropriate age. The great majority of children stop thumb sucking spontaneously as they get caught up in learning new skills and no longer need to be stimulated or comforted by sucking. A study by Dr. T. Berry Brazelton indicates that as many as 94 percent have finished with sucking their thumbs by their first birthdays.

According to the American Dental Association, thumb sucking does not cause permanent problems with the teeth or jawline unless it is continued beyond four to five years of age. Many studies have looked at the number of children who continue to suck their thumbs longer than that. As it turns out, somewhere between 85 and 99 percent of children have finished thumb sucking spontaneously before this period. When investigators studied children who sucked their thumbs beyond their first birthday, looking for common traits, they found one thing that distinguished late thumb suckers from other children—a prolonged history of a strong battle over thumb sucking at an earlier age. It is striking that many well-meaning parents have actually encouraged this behavior by forcibly trying to take the thumb out of their children's mouths.

For children in the first year of life, sucking to fall asleep or for comfort is self-limiting and wonderful. If they are sucking their thumbs simply because they are bored or "zoned out," it is a good idea to distract them by handing them something interesting to hold onto, without even mentioning their thumbs.

If your child has not spontaneously stopped thumb sucking by the time he is talking, there are ways to actively encourage him to stop. Right now, however, you do not need to be concerned about your child's natural way of getting the stimulation and comfort he needs in an independent and healthy way. If you find that the sight of his thumb sucking bothers you, you might want to offer him a pacifier to use until his sucking need diminishes at about nine months.

TOOTH CARE

It's never too early to get your child into the habit of taking care of his teeth. Even if the only teeth he now has are baby teeth (which he will eventually lose), he'll need them to chew his food for years to come.

Starting Good Oral Hygiene Habits
I was a dental assistant for years and saw many babies with decay—breastfed and bottle-fed. I used to give my daughter a toothbrush during her "tubby," starting when she was about eight months old. She would just chew on it then. But as she got older, I never had to fight her to get her teeth brushed.
~ *Monique G., Whately, Massachusetts*

I took my son to the dentist for a consultation when he was a year old. The dentist told us it was a good idea to have him drink a little water after eating or drinking if we couldn't brush right away, and that it would help rinse off the teeth.
~ *Suzanne L., Pasadena, California*

Keeping Teeth Clean

To clean baby's teeth, wet a thin, soft washcloth or gauze. Wrap the cloth around your finger and rub the teeth and gums with a gentle pressure. This works better than toothbrushes for babies eighteen months and younger.

~ *Noni B., Lafayette, Louisiana*

DR. GREENE'S INSIGHT

Baby-bottle tooth decay is the specific form of severe decay found in the teeth of infants and toddlers who fall asleep with a bottle of milk, juice, or any sweetened liquid in the mouth. It is the only severe dental disease common in children under three years of age.

Unlike adults' cavities, which are largely invisible, a baby's cavities caused by baby-bottle tooth decay are on the visible portion of the front teeth. The upper four central teeth are the ones affected. Their counterparts in the lower gum, protected by the tongue during sucking and washed by saliva, usually remain sound.

The process of tooth decay is quite gradual. Over time the teeth are weakened. Usually, the enamel is finally breached sometime between 12 and 18 months of age. The cavities first appear at the gum line as subtle, white, decalcified streaks. The process then begins to accelerate. In advanced cases, the crowns of the four upper incisors are completely destroyed, leaving decayed, brownish black stumps that distort the spacing of the permanent teeth. I have seen this many, many times.

When one falls asleep, saliva production decreases rapidly. Swallowing also decreases, and liquids present in the mouth at the time of falling asleep tend to pool for long periods. Your best bet is to move the bedtime bottle forward in time, so that your son is still awake 15 minutes after finishing. This will lessen any chances for his teeth to decay.

TOYS *(See also Guilt and Playing)*

If you are looking for the toy that will entertain your baby while you get a chance to clean the house or read a magazine, the parents on the Parent Soup message boards suggest that you may be looking a long time. One of the beautiful things about babies is that they don't care what the latest, greatest toys are (just wait a few years, and you may pine for these days). There is one toy that is mentioned over and over again on our boards—the Exersaucer, which is similar to a walker except that it isn't supposed to move. The Exersaucer's benefits are espoused in some of the posts below, and Dr. Greene steps in to give his input on the debate about whether babies should be placed in walkers.

Mom and Dad Are the Best Toys

Gadgets and toys can be a godsend for a busy mommy, and they can also be overused. But all that stuff is meaningless to a baby, whose favorite toy is mommy and daddy! I see all the posts saying, "My baby has this and that and is not content with it at all. What can I do?" I always smile because I remember feeling the same way. Now I know that babies don't give a fig what you buy. They want *you* to play with them, and they don't care if you have dinner or sleep or if the laundry gets done. Sometimes I get frustrated and think there are hundreds of dollars' worth of toys in their bedroom, and if they would just leave me alone for a little while, I could have the whole house clean. I have to *force* myself daily to remember that the cleaning and laundry will always be there, and my kids' youth will not. So I kick the dirty clothes out of the way and go play or read *Winnie the Pooh* aloud for the one-thousandth time.

~ *Angela K., South Bound Brook, New Jersey*

Don't go crazy with toys for newborns; they don't play but mostly just look at things. There's a lot of stuff out there designed to rip off new, confused, exhausted parents, I'm convinced. Your baby will just want to hear your voice and look at things. Look for a great book called *Entertain Me!* by the Riverside Mothers Group. It has lots of great ideas for fun for babies, words to songs and nursery rhymes, and more. A great purchase!

   ~ Cary O., Woodbridge, Virginia

Praise for the Exersaucer

There are three toys I couldn't do without for my daughter: the swing, the Fisher Price Sound and Lights Activity Gym, and the Exersaucer. The Exersaucer is, in my humble opinion, the second-greatest invention after the baby swing. When I first put her in the Exersaucer, there wasn't much of a reaction. But after about a week, all that changed. She is so content and loves all the toys on her tray. I almost didn't get one because they are a storage nightmare, but I decided we'll just donate it to a day-care center or something when she outgrows it.

   ~ Amy W., Greenwich, Connecticut

My storage solution for the Exersaucer is to keep loaning it out. It is only useful for a maximum of six months, so I just let all of my friends know when they have their babies that the Exersaucer is available for loan. A relief nursery or a lending library of baby equipment are also good places to donate one.

   ~ Tarrant F., Eugene, Oregon

The Great Walker Debate

I'm not an expert on walkers, but my daughter did have one. I wasn't sure about it, but it was given to me as a gift, and it turns out she loved it. It was very convenient while I was cooking in the kitchen, or doing the laundry, or whatever. She thought it was great! There have been many bad things said about walkers, mainly how babies can fall down the steps and injure themselves if they are in the walker. But then again, they can fall down the steps even out of a walker. It all depends on how you baby-proof your house.

~ *Susan N., Fairhope, Alabama*

Q: I have a nine-month-old boy who weighs 24 lb. and 6 oz. and is 31 inches long. Do you think that it is safe for him to be in a walker?

~ *Traci, South Carolina*

DR. GREENE'S INSIGHT

A: Children between six and twelve months old have a powerful urge to move across the floor. When they are placed in baby walkers, most of them squeal with delight and are happily entertained for hours on end. I can still remember the expression of sheer ecstasy on our first son's face as he moved across the floor in his walker.

We want our children to be happy. Often their delight is a good measure of what they need—but sometimes it can lead us astray. Sometimes short-term delight can lead to unfortunate long-term consequences. Since the days when my first son was an infant, for instance, we have learned that walkers are detrimental to normal development. Because the babies can get around too easily, their urge to move across the floor is satisfied, and many of them will not undertake the important tasks of crawling, creeping, scooting, or hitching. This stage is important for developing strength and coordination.

Many parents think that walkers will help children learn to walk. As it turns out, walkers interfere with learning to walk. In addition to decreasing the desire to walk by providing an easier alternative, walkers strengthen the wrong muscles. The lower legs are strengthened, but the upper legs and hips become relatively weak. The upper legs and hips are most important for walking.

Moreover, children in walkers have more accidents than their counterparts. Walkers often tip over when a child bumps into a small toy or the edge of a rug. Children in them are also more likely to take a dangerous fall down a flight of stairs. Along with the American Academy of Pediatrics, I strongly urge parents not to use baby walkers.

For children who want to be upright, an Exersaucer can be a nice alternative. These look like walkers, but without the wheels. They allow children to bounce, rock, spin, and sit upright—without satisfying the urge to move across the floor. They are safe and developmentally appropriate.

Your son might like a sturdy push-car or wagon. These might look like lawn mowers, vacuum cleaners, cars, fire engines, trucks, or simple wagons. Be sure it has a bar that he can push and is sturdy enough so it won't tip over. These will help a child strengthen the right muscles and learn to walk—but you still have to be very careful about stairs.

When your son gets a little older and has been walking long enough to be able to squat and stand back up without falling, he will be delighted by push-and-pull toys, especially the ones that make lots of noise. These add sparkle to his developmentally appropriate tasks.

With practice, you can learn to choose toys that delight your son while helping him learn what he needs—instead of short-circuiting the process by providing easy, numbing entertainment. We'll all make mistakes along the way, but the selection process itself will enrich us and our children.

TRAVEL—By Airplane

So you're ready to take the baby show on the road. How can you keep travel from turning into a stress-fest? Not only is it possible, but parents who have done it are here to tell you all the secret tricks of the trade, like how to get a seat for your baby without paying for it, how to quiet the baby who hates being in the car seat, and even how to navigate the subway with a baby in tow. So start packing already!

Taking the Stroller with You
Most of the smaller, umbrella-style strollers will fit in the overhead bins. Even if you can't fit it in the overhead, the airlines will let you check it at the gate, and it will be waiting for you at the plane door when you get off.
   ~ *Kathy H., Knoxville, Tennessee*

How to Get an Extra Seat Without Paying for It
If you have a young baby with a rear-facing car seat and you cannot afford the cost of a ticket, call the airline a day or two before your flight and ask if the flight has any open seats. If you find there are openings, take your car seat along. Ask the flight attendant when you board if she will help you switch seats with someone so that you're next to an empty seat. That way, you can use the empty seat for your baby free of charge.

I have never had a flight attendant refuse that request; they have all been happy to do it. If there are no empty seats, your infant seat will fit in the overhead compartment.

~ Sarah M., Cedar Falls, Iowa

When an Extra Seat Is Worth the Money

My advice, gained from dragging my 14-month-old across the planet, is to *buy a seat* for your baby. Also pack lots of new and exciting things for her to do (new books, toys). And make sure she has something to eat or drink during the takeoffs and landings: I swear by this—on flights where my husband and I have had severe ear pain, she has sat by blissfully.

~ Parent Soup member Dwf96

We ask for an aisle and a window seat so that the center seat might possibly be open (hardly anyone ever requests a center seat).

~ Parent Soup member PEETIEBEAN

Breastfeeding on the Plane

I found that I would get looks from other passengers when I tried to breastfeed my baby on the plane. I started carrying two safety pins in my diaper bag—they were all I needed to keep everyone, including the baby, happy. First, get a window seat and one of the airline blankets. Use the safety pins to attach the blanket to the top of the seat in front of you and to the top of the seat you are in, creating a wall between you and them. This way, you can be more comfortable, and the baby doesn't have to be totally covered with a blanket when he or she is trying to eat. This also makes your space a little darker and the baby is more apt to sleep.

~ Barbara W., Andover, New Jersey

Earache Rx

My husband and I traveled by plane to North Carolina when our son was only five months. My doctor recommended that a half hour before the flight we give the baby Tylenol and a decongestant. This prevented his ears from clogging and hurting him. It also made him very sleepy. He slept almost the whole flight until we were ready to land.

~ *Val W., Mercer Island, Washington*

Why Younger Babies Are Better Travelers

I found traveling with kids under four months the easiest time to travel with them. They sleep a lot and they don't need to move around much. I would try not to nurse the baby for a while before takeoff and landing so that she would be hungry enough to nurse during those times. It's good for the baby's ears if she is sucking during those changes in altitudes.

~ *Emily, New York*

> **DR. GREENE'S INSIGHT:** Swallowing, not just sucking, during descent is especially important (not so much for takeoff). As the plane goes up, the air in the middle ear expands, and the ears pop automatically. During descent, when the middle ear needs some extra air to equilibrate, the baby must swallow, yawn, or cry to open the floppy eustachian tube.

When to Get off the Plane

When you deplane, wait for everyone else to get off first. This may take an extra 10 minutes, but you'll be much more calm and collected before the mad rush to the baggage terminal (only to have to wait for another 15 or more minutes for your luggage).

~ *Monique N., Hermosa Beach, California*

TRAVEL—By Car

When They Hate Facing Backward

For a baby who screams when you put her in a rear-facing car seat, my best advice is to sit with her in the back seat. Bring along plenty of toys, books, and so on. If you're nursing, you can lean over the seat and nurse her while she's still safely strapped inside. Yes, it does qualify you as a world-class gymnast, but it's doable. If nothing works and she still screams, you'll just have to make up your mind that there are going to be a lot of stops along the way. I remember one trip my husband and I took when our middle boy was an infant. What should have taken us three hours took us just over seven! We stopped a lot, had two nice meals out while on the road, and arrived with a relatively happy child. We were pretty relaxed, too—just tired.

~ *Wendy, California*

My baby hated being in a car seat when she had to be rear-facing. She couldn't see out the windows and couldn't see Mom when I was driving. I put one of those crib mirrors on the back seat and positioned it so she could see me when I was driving. It was amazing how she calmed down after that. Now that she's facing forward, it isn't as much of a problem. But we do keep small toys and graham crackers available to hand back to her to keep her happier.

~ *Susan W., Covina, California*

Have you tried giving her a pacifier while she's in a car seat? That often works for us.

~ *Parent Soup member Ksteinken*

TRIVIA QUESTION

When did the U.S government require that all car seats be crash-tested?

a. 1976

b. 1990

c. 1981

d. 1968

e. 1984

Answer: c

Before 1981 many car seats were independently tested, but there was no national measure.

We've also discovered that getting our son out of his car seat to be held and played with at the rest stop works wonders. He gets to wiggle and stretch.

~ *Tara L., Augusta, Georgia*

Take Advantage of Their Confinement

Does your child put up a fight when it's time to cut his nails? Try cutting his nails right after you put him in his car seat. When he's already strapped in, you may have better luck!

~ *Monica H., Evanston, Illinois*

Breastfeeding on the Go

I've had to breastfeed my baby on the road many times. It's pretty easy on you when your baby is in a rear-facing car seat. When the seat is facing forward, just use some pillows to protect your ribs, maybe a blanket so as not to cause an accident, and you and the baby will get the job done.

~ *Wendy, California*

I tried to pump in the car while riding when I was on a road trip with my husband and our four-month-old daughter. But it was uncomfortable and so slow that the baby was getting jealous of the pump. So I just leaned over and let her nurse from her seat. It was fairly uncomfortable, but it quieted her until we could pull over.

~ *Tasha S., Coconut Creek, Florida*

Take Your Own Car Seat, Even If You're Renting a Car

Be careful if you are counting on renting the car seat from the car rental agency. They may not have any more (then what do you do?) or the one

From *Parent Soup: The Game*

they offer may be damaged or inadequate or just plain scuzzy. Best to bring your own.

~ *Anne L., Cedar Rapids, Iowa*

Testing the Nighttime Waters

It's one idea to take a car trip at night so your baby will sleep on the way, but we tried it a couple of times and it was miserable. He wouldn't calm down, no matter what we did (including stopping). If you haven't already done so, I would take him for a spin in the car near bedtime and see what happens. It helps on car trips if we stock up with lots of toys, books, and tapes. We also make sure to give our son enough time to run around during breaks; if we put him back in the car too soon, he gets really mad.

~ *Suzanne L., Pasadena, California*

Alleviating Car Sickness

For a baby that gets carsick, put the car seat in the middle of the back seat so he can see out the front window. Also, make sure the window is cracked so he gets some fresh air. And the best activity is stories and music on tapes so he isn't trying to focus on anything.

~ *Emily, New York*

TRAVEL—By Train

Consider the Train for a Less Stressful Trip

I took my five-month-old on Amtrak from Washington, D.C., to Orlando, Florida, and it worked out great! I was afraid to take her on a plane because she still cried a lot, and I thought it would be too stressful.

I took an overnight train and got a sleeping compartment. The train left D.C. at 8:30 P.M. My daughter spent about an hour examining the room and hallway. Then I fed her and she went to sleep. I put her on the bed between myself and the wall. She woke up once during the night but slept through until 6:30 A.M. We had breakfast and then wandered around on the train. We also got off the train during longer stops. We pulled into Orlando at 1 P.M., refreshed and ready to go. There were a couple different types of sleeping compartments. I found the best was the one with a long sofa that converts into a bed; it had more legroom for a baby to sit or crawl, and the bed was flush against the wall (no gaps to get caught in). Also, the porter was very helpful with handling baggage, making up the bed, and bringing meals into the room.

~ *Desma C., Germantown, Maryland*

Braving the Subway

I live in New York and always take my baby in the subways (although the noise level is a bit upsetting in some places). Try a Baby Bjorn or similar front carrier, a backpack, or, even better, a sling. If you still need a stroller, put her in a sling while navigating the steps. I have almost always found people who offer to help me up or down the stairs with the stroller. I carry a toy whistle for the times when I need to get the token booth attendant's attention to open the gate, although usually someone else will make the request for me before I get into gear! She's more portable now, so I suggest going sans stroller and avoiding the hassle. Remember to lock the brakes on the stroller once you're settled in the train!

~ *Simone W., New York, New York*

TRAVEL—General Tips

Making Long Trips a Little Easier
I work for the airlines and had to fly from Los Angeles to New York when my baby was four months old. Here are some suggestions I hope you can use:

1. Ship necessities via Federal Express. It's not cheap, but they get there the very next day. I just packed all my stuff and sent it off the day before I left.

2. If you stay at a hotel, see if it offers child-friendly amenities, such as portacribs and high chairs. Call before you get there or, better yet, when you're booking the room.

3. If you're staying with friends or relatives, ask them if they (or friends of theirs) have children's stuff you can borrow for the duration of your stay.

4. Call the chamber of commerce in the city you plan to visit to see if they have businesses that rent baby equipment.

5. If you need a car seat, Midas Mufflers has a great safety program available for new car seats. For $40 you can buy a brand-new Century 1000 car seat. When you're done with it, return it to any Midas shop and receive $40 in brakes or muffler service. If you're visiting friends or relatives, have them get it for you before you get there, so it can be in the car when they pick you up.

6. A portable play yard can't be beat. We got an Evenflo Happy Cabana. They finally make an insert that acts as a bassinet. It folds down into its own travel bag. I can set mine up in minutes by myself.

7. One last thing I find indispensable is a folding chair that attaches to a table to put the baby at your level to feed him. This will work if your baby is old enough to sit up. We also had a plastic folding chair that can double as a bath seat.
   ~ *Monique N., Hermosa Beach, California*

A Car Seat for Car to Plane and Back Again

The *best* car seat for travel (airplanes, switching vehicles, etc.) is Safeline's Sit & Stroll. Besides being a comfortable and safe seat, it has built-in wheels that fold up into the seat (like landing gear) by moving a lever. There's also a retractable handle. You have no extra stroller to lug or stow! Imagine being able to have this seat in the car, roll it through the airport and onto the plane, and plop it into the seat, all without unstrapping your child! This seat has a rear-facing range of 5 to 32 pounds and a forward-facing one of 20 to 40 pounds. The car or plane seatbelt goes *over* the seat, which makes installation especially fast and secure in travel situations. This seat has served us so well that we never found the need to purchase a separate stroller.
   ~ *Michelle, Texas*

If You Won't Be Near a Laundromat

When I travel with our kids, I usually take along a small bottle of dish detergent and a combo nipple-and-bottle brush that folds in half, so I can

PARENT POLL

What age would your child have to be for you to leave him with a
relative or baby-sitter for a week so you could go on vacation?

Of 975 total votes

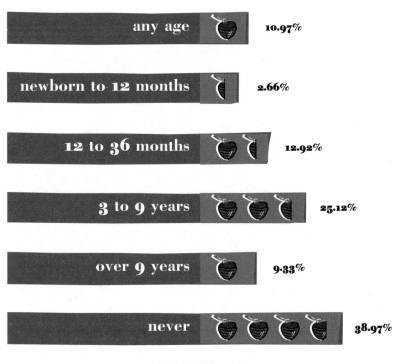

any age	10.97%
newborn to 12 months	2.66%
12 to 36 months	12.92%
3 to 9 years	25.12%
over 9 years	9.33%
never	38.97%

1 bowl = 100 parents

wash out the bottles at night. The water will get hot enough in the sink for this. The detergent also comes in handy if I need to hand-wash something.

~ *Andrea B., Ft. Lauderdale, Florida*

Hotel Baby-Sitters
Most of the major hotels have baby-sitters. They will come to your hotel room, and they are trustworthy, since the hotel wouldn't want to end up in trouble for something the sitter did. We used a sitter service in Orlando when our baby was 14 months. She came to the room, and I left a schedule of what his day normally was like, when he ate, and the phone number of where we'd be.

~ *Silvia W., Las Vegas, Nevada*

WALKERS *(See Toys)*

WEANING

Weaning your baby means so much more than making the transition to a cup: you have less cuddle time built into your day, but you have more independence. If you've been breastfeeding, the chances are you're leaking like crazy (turn to pages 28–30 for help with that), and if you have been bottle-feeding, you're probably rejoicing that you'll never have to wash another bottle again (until you have another child). But the most amazing thing is that your baby is starting to look a little less like an infant and a little more like toddler. How did it happen so fast?

From the Breast

● **To Relieve the Engorgement and Pain of Weaning**
Try some cabbage leaves! I know it sounds strange, but I'm serious. It's been proved that there's an astringent in cabbage leaves that reduces swelling and engorgement. Chill or freeze some cabbage leaves. Crush them a little, then put one over each breast. This can also be used to reduce postpartum engorgement, but unless you are not breastfeeding, be careful, because the leaves can reduce your milk supply if you leave them on too long.
    ~ *Angie B., Durand, Michigan*

● **Dealing with Plugged Ducts**
I had plugged ducts frequently with my first baby. They can be very painful and may occur following weaning if your breasts are still producing milk and not being emptied, or if you wean too fast. You need to pump to keep the breast empty. Then you can wean yourself from the pump to decrease any milk production.
    ~ *Faye D., Hammond, Indiana*

From the Bottle

● **Involve Your Child in the Process**
This is what I did with my oldest son. I know it won't work for a lot of kids, but it was perfect with him. After he got used to drinking from his

269

cup, I had *him* take all of his bottles and put them in a trash bag. Then I walked him to the garbage can, where he put them. He didn't miss them until it was time for his "nite-nite" bottle. I explained to him what he did so he could be a big boy. He did cry for the first few nights, but it wasn't too bad.

~ *Jennifer G., Salt Lake City, Utah*

● **Switch Bottles**

I had success by switching my son to a sports water bottle—one with the spout you suck on, not the straw. Another idea, is to try giving only water in the bottle and milk or juice from a cup.

~ *Parent Soup member MNKYDU*

Introducing a Cup

● **Making the Transition Easier**

When giving your baby a sipper cup for the first time, put juice in it instead of formula or breast milk. Babies tend to associate milk with sucking from a nipple and may be more likely to try to drink from a cup if it contains juice.

~*Noni B., Lafayette, Louisiana*

index